Classic Composers

Published by Magna Books, Magna Road, Wigston, Leicester, LE8 2ZH, England

© 1991 Gruppo Editoriale Fabbri S. p. A. Milan

Concept and production by Gruppo Editoriale Fabbri according
to a proposal from Euredition, Den Haag.

Editions of this book will appear simultaneously in France,
Germany, Great Britain, Italy, the Netherlands and Sweden
under the auspices of Euredition, Den Haag.

Texts by Anna Maria Mascheroni, G Marchesi, Alberta Melanotte,
C. Orselli, Eduardo Rescigno and Rubens Tedeschi.
English translation by Stephan Thorne.
Layout: Barbara Ravera
Typesetting: Buro AD, Amersfoort
Printed in Italy by Gruppo Editoriale Fabbri S.p.A. Milan.

© S.I.A.E. 1991, Rome, for the works of Alexandre Benois (p. 157, 176),
Daniel Louradbour (p. 159), Jacques-Emile Blanche (p. 167, 173), Leon Bakst
(p. 168, 170, 174, 175), Jean Cocteau (p. 177, 178), Pablo Picasso (p. 178).
Photo credits: Archives of Gruppo Editoriale Fabbri, Milan

ISBN 185422 2465

Classic Composers

MAGNA BOOKS

Contents

Introduction

Opportunities to hear classical music are increasing daily. Concerts are crowded out, younger listeners are rediscovering opera, and even large halls cannot accommodate the 'fans' who flock there to hear their favourite soloists. Moreover, cinema and television have not been slow to realise that changes in habit and taste on such a scale cannot easily be ignored. And yet, even today, the great figures of music history can still surprise us.

The aim of this Dictionary is to offer those who already enjoy classical music a series of 'encounters' with some of the greatest musicians of all time, from Vivaldi and Bach to Debussy and Stravinsky, but in such a way that their enjoyment and knowledge of music will be enriched still further. Full biographies are provided, with the explicit intention of dispelling the aura of mystery that legend has often wrapped around the great musicians of the past and these are augmented by a wealth of illustrations to give an idea of what it meant to be a composer, what the composer's 'trade' involved. Thus, we see that composing, like any other profession, had its own practical and human problems and implied the same endless search for a distinctive idiom or style that could set any given musical practitioner apart from his predecessors or contemporary rivals.

The composer who now seems to have been free to follow his own creative impulse was, in fact, bound first to the patron or client – whether nobleman or prince of the church – who commissioned his work, and then to the impresario who arranged for it to be performed and the critics who listened to it. The needs of prima donna singers and court players also had to be taken into account, musical instruments were constantly evolving and changing, music printing was still in its infancy, and distribution of musical texts was still a difficult business.

This representative selection of portraits amounts, in fact, to a brief though fully authoritative history of music in which the lives of individual composers illustrate how the relationship between musicians and their public has evolved over the centuries. As it moves chronologically from the eighteenth century of Bach, Vivaldi and Handel to the twentieth century, with Debussy, Stravinsky and Gershwin, the Dictionary relates the personality and output of each composer to the development of his own style and assesses the contribution this has made to the evolution of Western music in general.

We hope that readers will find this Dictionary a useful way of enriching their enjoyment and knowledge of music.

Interior of the church of St. Michael at Lüneburg. Lüneburg Museum.

Bach

Portrait of Johann Sebastian Bach as a young man by an unknown 18th-century artist. Anger Museum, Erfurt.

Johann Sebastian Bach was born at Eisenach in Thuringia on 21 March 1685. When his father died very young and scarcely a year after his mother, the orphaned boy, only ten years old and the youngest of eight children, was obliged to leave his native town, where he had been attending the local school for the past three years, to live in Ohrdruf with his elder brother Johann Christoph, organist in the Michaelskirche. There he completed the Latin studies he had begun in Eisenach, studied music with his brother, went to the local lyceum and sang in the *chorus musicus*. Above all, he showed a great desire to learn everything very quickly.

In 1700, at the age of 15, Bach moved to Lüneburg, a town south of Hamburg, to study at the Michaelsschule, where he became thoroughly acquainted with the German polyphonic tradition which had just begun to feel the influence of French music. These years were crucial to his musical education: new horizons were opened up to him, and he began to look further afield to the great organ schools of northern Germany. He went to Hamburg and from there to Celle, a tiny principality governed by a French princess. In its small though refined court the young student became acquainted with French harpsichord music, with the result that the ornaments and graces of composers such as Couperin, Raison and Dieupart were added to his store of musical resources.

Other important journeys were made. After working as a violinist in Weimar (which he had visited for the first time), Bach moved on to Arnstadt

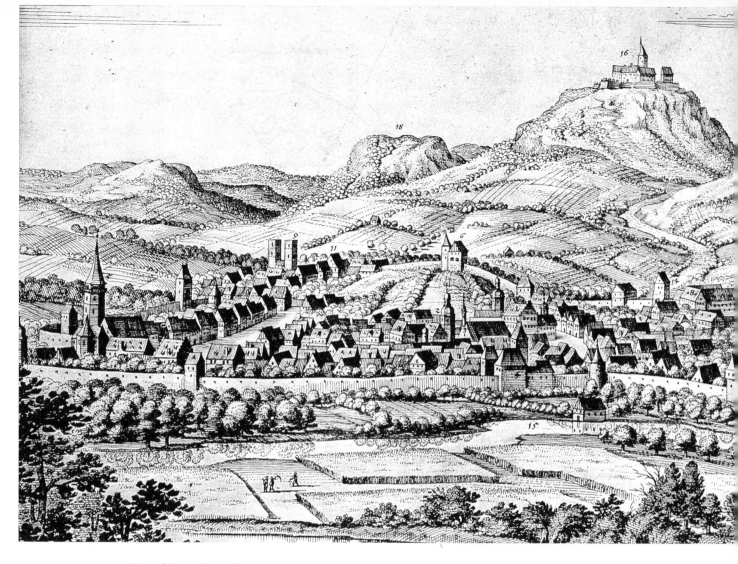

View of Eisenach in Thuringia, Bach's native town. Engraving. Deutsche Fotothek, Dresden.

where he played the organ in the Neukirche. In Lübeck he heard Buxtehude, southern Germany's most celebrated organist.

From Arnstadt, Bach moved to Mühlhausen in 1707 to become organist in the Church of St Blasius, where his duties included the performing of cantatas, or 'regulated sacred music' as they were then called. His earliest surviving cantatas and some organ pieces date from this period. In the same year he married his cousin Maria Barbara, who subsequently bore him seven children (only four of whom survived infancy, however). Two of them, Wilhelm Friedemann ('Bach of Halle') and Carl Philipp Emanuel ('Bach of Hamburg') became important musical figures in their own right.

Bach stayed only a few months in Mühlhausen, and in the summer of 1708 we find him in Weimar at the court of Duke Wilhelm Ernst of Weimar-Saxony, in a new post that was neither well paid nor especially prestigious. His duties included playing the organ in the castle, and violin in the nobleman's 16-piece chamber orchestra, but the

post was good enough, and he was appointed *Konzertmeister* in 1714. The Duke was a keen musician, and loved playing in his orchestra and composing under the guidance of his tutor, the highly respected Johann Gottfried Walther, a distant relative of Bach himself, who had travelled extensively and was well acquainted with the Italian concerto repertoire of his day (Corelli, Vivaldi, Albinoni). Walther passed his love of Italian concertos on to the Duke, which explains why Italian music, especially Vivaldi, was particularly popular at his court. Obviously, Bach too began to take an interest in this repertoire, and his desire to know more about music that was new in Germany at the time resulted in a number of transcriptions of Italian instrumental pieces for keyboard. Those that have survived are organ and harpsichord pieces transcribed from works by Vivaldi, Alessandro Marcello and Albinoni. In addition to writing music for general court entertainment (serenades and secular cantatas, including the remarkable *Jagdkantate*), Bach also had to compose sacred music and play the castle church organ, which was completely overhauled and enlarged during his stay there, possibly at his own suggestion. After respecification, its enhanced range of colour and volume was incorporated into many of his later organ works.

In fact, most of Bach's organ works were written in Weimar (the great preludes, fugues and toccatas, including the famous Toccata in D minor), and he must have spent much time writing cantatas for church services. He also had a large number of pupils, for whom he began to write the 45 chorales of his famous *Orgelbüchlein* (Little organ book).

The Duke's *Kapellmeister* died in 1716, and Bach felt that he had a rightful claim to his position, but in the event he was passed over. Relations between Bach and his patron were strained, and he asked to resign, but the Duke at first refused. When, in late 1717, he succeeded in leaving Weimar, Bach went immediately to work for Prince Leopold of Anhalt-Cöthen. In doing so, he effectively ceased to be a professional organist. From then on, he worked either as a *Kapellmeister* (in Cöthen) or, later, a *Kantor* (in Leipzig).

Although relatively short, Bach's stay in Cöthen from late 1717 to early 1723 was extremely important. His composing was channelled in new direc-

Portrait of Duke Wilhelm Ernst of Saxon-Weimar. Rococo-Museum, Weimar.

tions because in the Prince's Calvinist court there was little interest in sacred music (cantatas and chorales). Accordingly, the composer concentrated on chamber and orchestral composition, with the result that we now have the important sonatas and partitas for solo violin, the suites for solo cello, the sonatas for violin and harpsichord, the two Violin Concertos and the overtures for orchestra. Bach also became increasingly interested in the harpsichord, completing both the first book of the *Well-tempered clavier* and the famous *Chromatic fantasy and fugue*. Bach wrote (or was able to write) only a few cantatas, but he did compose the first of his two great passions, the *St John passion*, which was performed in Leipzig on 26 March 1723.

In effect, then, Bach was obliged to widen his musical and composing horizons at Cöthen: as *Kapellmeister*, he was responsible for all the music played at court. In addition, he had to keep the Prince's music library up to date, himself copy or have copied all the interesting new music that came his way, and buy new instruments for the court orchestra in which the Prince himself played. He also had to accompany the Prince on his travels. While in Karlsbad on one such journey, Bach met Christian Ludwig, the Margrave of Brandenburg. Meeting him again a year later in Berlin, he was commissioned to write six concertos, possibly as a result of musical conversations with the Margrave,

The only known portrait of Johann Ambrosius Bach, father of Johann Sebastian. Deutsche Staatsbibliothek, Berlin.

although we cannot be sure. What is certain is that the sixth *Brandenburg Concerto* was written then, and the third and second a few months later. These six masterly concertos dedicated to the Margrave Christian Ludwig are now known collectively as the *Brandenburg Concertos*.

Bach himself also travelled widely during his stay at Cöthen. He was called to Leipzig to supervise work on the organ in St Paul's Church there, and in 1719 we find him in Halle and, once again, in Karlsbad. On his return in 1720 he learned that his wife had died during his absence. Grief-stricken, he found himself with a young family to bring up and provide for. On 21 December the following year Bach married Anna Magdalena Wilke who was to bear him 13 children (again, many died in infancy). Anna Magdalena knew music, played the harpsichord well and had a fine voice, and Bach wrote pieces for harpsichord, clavichord and chamber organ for her and her children. The *Notebook* of 1722 was dedicated to Anna Magdalena, as well as another composed in 1725.

Bach's duties as **Kapellmeister** at Cöthen were drastically reduced by Leopold's marriage to his young cousin Friderica Henrietta of Anhalt-Bern-

A German "collegium musicum" in an 18th-century engraving. Civica Raccolta di Stampe Bertarelli, Milan.

The title page of Bach's "Orgelbüchlein". Deutsche Staatsbibliothek, Berlin.

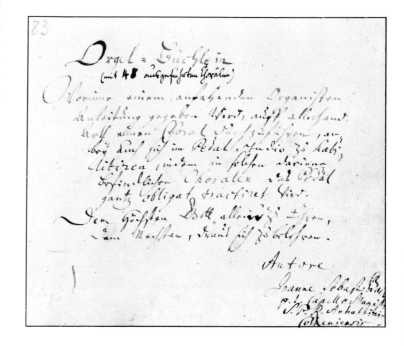

Page of a manuscript of a Bach choral. Autograph z.Z.,
Universitäsbibliothek, Tubingen.

burg. She was uncultured and had little interest in
the arts (she disliked music especially), and Bach
soon realised that he would have to start looking
for another post. He turned his attention towards
Leipzig, a Lutheran city in the Electorate of Saxony
where there was a famous university with two
collegia musica, and a fine opera house. Leipzig
was also famous throughout Europe as a Humanist
city, and so it seemed the ideal place in which to
have his children educated (he dreamed of giving
them a better education than he had received).
Moreover, the post of *Kantor* at the famous Thomasschule was vacant. Johann Kuhnau, the previous *Kantor* and a fine composer, had died in June
1722, and so Bach applied for the post when it was
advertised in February 1723. He was examined, his
two test cantatas were performed, and on 19 April
he accepted the terms of the contract. A *Kantor* had
lower status than a *Kapellmeister*, but Leipzig itself was a strong attraction: its musical life was le-
gendary and its cultural importance was unques-
tionable. His paid work began on 15 May 1723, but
he was already fairly well known in Leipzig because a performance of his *St John passion* in March
that year (appropriately enough in the Thomaskirche) had been well received.

The duties of the Thomasschule *Kantor* were closely linked to the work of its sister institution, the
Thomaskirche, because the school's pupils were
highly sought after for religious and musical cere-
monies in Leipzig. The best ones formed the choirs
of the city's two main churches, St Thomas and St
Nicholas, and were trained by the *Kantor* himself.
Bach was thus obliged to write religious music
whenever a religious service or ceremony required
it, and this meant not just large-scale works such as
the Magnificats or passions, but also the cantatas
that were needed for services every Sunday. Bach
wrote several hundred of them, of which 195 sur-
vive, almost certainly written in Leipzig.

During this period Bach wrote an enormous
amount, but that was not unusual for a composer of
his time in his position. More than the sheer quantity of his work, however, it is its consistent quality
that is truly astonishing, for his life-long study of
polyphonic technique culminated in Leipzig in the
great cantatas, oratorios (such as the famous
Christmas oratorio) and passions. He wrote five
passions, but only two, the *St John passion* and the
St Matthew passion, have survived intact.

It might well be thought that Bach led a quiet, hard-
working life in Leipzig, on good terms with the authorities who had made him *Kantor*, but we know
from several sources, including his own letters,
that this was not so. Mutual incomprehension with
the authorities, arguments with singers and bad
feeling with the rector of the Thomasschule all aggravated what had never been a particularly easy-
going temperament.

As before, Bach travelled widely from his base in
Leipzig, giving concerts, trying out new organs or

Portrait of J.S. Bach. J.J. Ihle, 1720. Bach-Haus, Eisenach.

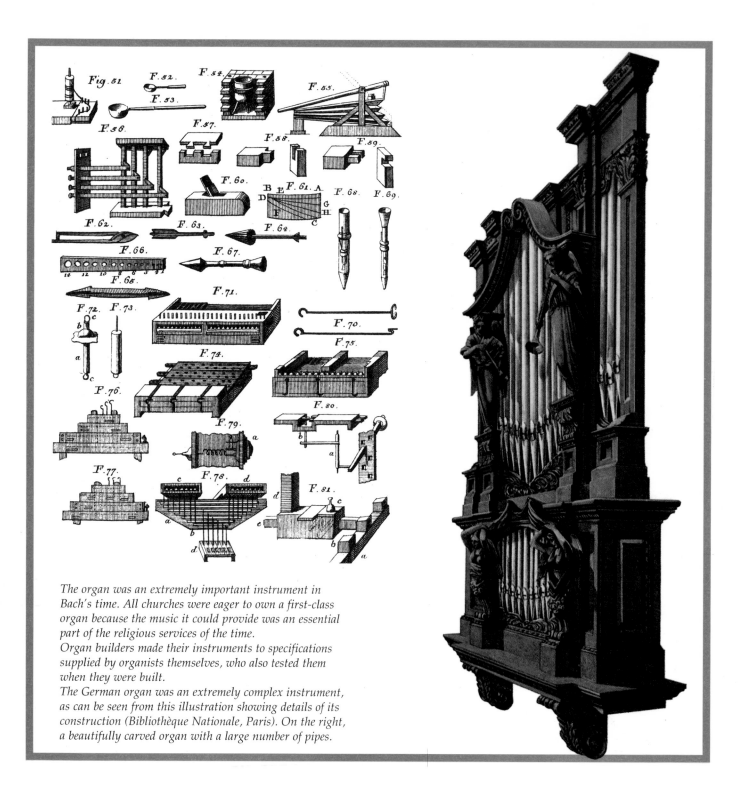

The organ was an extremely important instrument in Bach's time. All churches were eager to own a first-class organ because the music it could provide was an essential part of the religious services of the time.
Organ builders made their instruments to specifications supplied by organists themselves, who also tested them when they were built.
The German organ was an extremely complex instrument, as can be seen from this illustration showing details of its construction (Bibliothèque Nationale, Paris). On the right, a beautifully carved organ with a large number of pipes.

visiting his children who were now grown up and living in other cities. In the summer of 1741 he was in Berlin as the guest of his son Carl Philipp who was in service at the Prussian court. Returning there a few years later Bach was able to meet King Frederick II of Prussia. From local newspaper reports of May 1741, we know that the King gave Bach a theme and asked him to compose a fugue on it, and that the ageing composer improvised the fugue on the spot. On returning to Leipzig, this theme, reworked in a series of canons and *ricercari* and a trio sonata, became the basis of one of his most famous works, *A musical offering*, which Bach sent to the King with his dedication.

His final, extremely creative years produced, among other things, the *Canon variations on a Christmas cho-*

rale, an organ piece, and the famous *Art of fugue* – a set of contrapuntal studies for an unspecified keyboard instrument in which Bach distils a lifetime's knowledge of counterpoint and polyphony.

Suffering now from deteriorating eyesight, Bach underwent two eye operations early in 1750, which only seemed to make matters worse. He died in Weimar on 28 July 1750, almost totally blind.

His children and pupils remained, however, as well as the huge bulk of his work itself which has continuously irrigated the musical terrain through which it has flowed like an immense underground river, mysteriously reappearing in spatially or temporally remote locations in the form of countless natural musical springs. It is significant in itself that the tireless efforts of musicians and scholars in tracking down all the many derivatives of Bach's work to their ultimate source in his own compositions actually gave rise to a new discipline, musicology.

View of Leipzig in 1749 with the church of St. Thomas. Engraving. Bach-Archiv, Leipzig.

Vocal		

Sacred

	Mass in B minor	1733
	4 short masses	1737-38
	5 Sanctus	1723-50
	1 Christe Eleison	?
	1 Magnificat (2 versions)	1723 and 1728-31

oratorios & passions		
	Christmas Oratorio	1734
	Ascension Oratorio	1735
	Easter Oratorio	1736
	St. John Passion	1722-23
	St. Matthew Passion	1728-29
	St. Luke Passion (doubtful)	–
	St. Mark Passion (lost)	1731

approx. 10 motets		1723-37

approx. 350 chorales		pub. 1784-87

approx. 300 cantatas (approx. 230 survive)	including:	
	Aus der Tiefe BWV 131	1707
	Gottes Zeit BWV 106 (Actus tragicus)	1707
	Gott ist mein König BWV 71	1708
	Herz und Mund BWV 147	1716
	Die Himmel erzählen BWV 76	1723
	O Ewigkeit BWV 60	1723
	Siehe zu BWV 179	1723
	Du Hirte Israel BWV 104	1724
	Am Abend aber BWV 42	1725
	Ich bin ein guter Hirt BWV 85	1725
	Bisher habt ihr BWV 87	1725
	Man singet mit Freuden BWV 149	1728c
	Wachet auf BWV 140	1731
	Eine feste Burg BWV 80	1734-50

Secular

approx. 50 cantatas	including:	
	Was mir behagt BWV 208 (hunting cantata)	1713
	Durchlaucht'ser Leopold BWV 173a (serenade)	1717-23c
	Pastoral Cantata BWV 249a	1725
	The Happy Eolus BWV 205	1725
	Lass Fürstin, lass noch BWV 198	1727
	The Contest of Phoebe and Pan BWV 201	1729c
	Non so che sia dolore BWV 209	1729c
	Coffee Cantata BWV 211	1732-35c
	Hercules at the Fork BWV 213	1733
	O holder Tag, erwünschte Zeit BWV 210	1733
	Peasants' Cantata BWV 212	1742
	Amore traditore BWV 203	?

arias, songs etc.		
	arias (approx. 10) from the Anna Magdalena Notebook	1725-31
	Spiritual songs (approx. 70)	pub. 1736
	5 spiritual songs	?
	Quodlibet for a marriage (fragments)	1707?

Instrumental		

orchestral		
	5 overtures (or suites)	1721-36?
	6 Brandenburg Concertos	1721

concertos		
	13 concertos for 1/2/3/4 harpsichords & strings	1727-33
	3 concertos for 1 and 2 violins and strings	1720c
	1 triple concerto for flute, violin and cello	1730

chamber		
	3 sonatas and 3 partitas for solo violin	1720c
	6 suites for solo cello	1720c
	1 partita for solo flute	1720c
	6 sonatas for violin and harpsichord	1720c
	1 suite for violin and harpsichord	1720c
	1 fugue for violin and harpsichord	1720c
	1 sonata for 2 violins and basso continuo	1720c
	3 sonatas for viola da gamba & basso continuo	1720c
	6 Sonatas for flute and harpsichord	1720c
	1 Sonata for flute and basso continuo	1720c
	1 sonata for 3 flutes and basso continuo	1720c

lute		
	1 fugue	1720c
	1 prelude	1720-21
	3 suites	1720-22c
	1 partita	1722c
	1 prelude, fugue and allegro	?

harpsichord		
	Capriccio sopra la lontananza del suo fratello dilettissimo (Capriccio on the departure of his beloved brother)	1704
	Klavierbüchlein für Wilhelm Friedemann Bach	1720
	Chromatic Fantasia and Fugue in D minor	1720c
	6 English Suites and 6 French Suites	1720-22
	Klavierbüchlein für Anna Madalena Bach (2 vols.)	1722 & 1727
	15 Two-Part Inventions	1720-23
	15 Three-Part Symphonies	1720-23
	The Well-Tempered Clavier (Books 1 & 2)	1722 & 1744
	Klavierübung (6 partitas, 1 overture, Italian Concerto, 4 Duets, Goldberg Variations)	1725-42?
	16 concertos (transcriptions from Vivaldi, Alessandro Marcello, Telemann & others)	1708-17?

organ		
	37 partitas	1700-10
	1 Pastoral	1703-07
	22 variations	1705-47c
	22 Preludes and Fugues (Toccatas, Fantasias)	1709-39
	Orgel-Büchlein (46 chorales)	1708-23
	approx. 250 other chorales	1708-49
	1 Passacaglia	1716-17
	6 sonatas	1727c
	Small Harmonic Labyrinth (doubtful)	?
	6 concertos (trans. from Vivaldi & others)	1708-17

Canons		
	7 canons (2,3,4,6,7 & 8 parts)	1713?-49
	Musical Offering	1747
	Art of Fugue	1749-50

Vivaldi

Probable portrait of Antonio Vivaldi by an unknown artist. Civico Museo Bibliografico Musicale, Bologna.

'The Red Priest who plays the violin' is how Vivaldi was known in eighteenth-century Venice. We know relatively little about his life, and what we do know is often contradictory. He was born in 1678 and was christened two months after his birth because of a serious illness, perhaps the 'tightness in the chest' he referred to throughout his life. His father, Giovan Battista, was (so one document tells us) a *sona-dor* of the violin in the Basilica of St Mark. His mother, Camilla Calicchio, was a tailor's daughter. Little is known about Vivaldi's musical education. His father was probably his first teacher, but it is uncertain whether he was ever taught by Giovanni Legrenzi, the chorus master of St Mark's. The Vivaldi family was not a wealthy one, and Antonio was immediately marked down for the priesthood.

He was ordained on 24 March 1703, but only six months later was exonerated from giving Mass, although he continued to wear his priest's vestments. This gave rise to endless speculation and gossip in the decadent world of eighteenth-century Venice, and helped to start a whole series of legends about the 'Red Priest' (so called on account of his red hair). However, Vivaldi gave his own explanation in a letter to the Marchese Bentivoglio in 1737: 'I haven't said Mass for twenty-five years and never shall again, not because I'm forbidden to do so, but from my own choice, on account of an illness I suffered as a child'.

Freed from onerous ecclesiastical duties, Vivaldi was able to pursue his musical interests more fully. His career was immediate and rapid, perhaps helped by the fact that he was a priest. By September 1703 he was already 'violin and chorusmaster'

"Le orfanelle filharmoniche" ("philharmonic orphan girls") of Venice in a watercolour by Grevenbroech, 1700. Alte Pinakothek, Munich.

at the musical seminary of the Hospice of the Pietà in Venice, one of the city's most famous orphanages. In fact, all Venetian orphanages had the privilege of teaching music to the orphan girls in their care. The well-known **putte**, or 'philharmonic orphans' as they were also called, gave public choral and instrumental concerts in Venice on Sundays and Feast days. A document of 1749 says: 'They sing like angels and play the violin, the organ and all the other instruments'. Vivaldi was happy, and enjoyed being both a teacher and a performer. Most of all, he enjoyed composing, and it would seem likely that much of the music performed at the Pietà was composed by Vivaldi himself.

Vivaldi was an unpredictable man, and this is also true of his music, which is unsystematic and difficult to catalogue. Establishing the chronology of his works is a complicated business indeed. The first major point of reference is the printing in Venice of his 12 Chamber Sonatas, Op. 1, in 1705, followed in 1709, again in Venice, by his Sonatas for violin and bass, Op. 2. These two collections were later reprinted in Amsterdam (Op. 1 in 1709, Op. 2 in 1712), but we do not know exactly when they were composed. The important point was that his name was in print and that his works, especially those printed in Holland, were beginning to circulate in Europe.

Another collection, the concertos collectively known as the *Estro armonico* (Musical fancy), Op. 3, was printed in Amsterdam by Estienne Roger, a famous publisher of the time. Again there is controversy over exactly when they were composed, and we do not even know when the score was sent for printing because the publisher marked the pages with numbers only. However, we do know that the originality and sheer genius of Vivaldi's music took Europe by storm. Johann Sebastian Bach found his music particularly attractive: in far-off Weimar he transcribed for the keyboard (imaginatively rather than literally) a number of Vivaldi's instrumental concertos.

Vivaldi's relations with the Pietà in Venice cannot have been particularly good since he was suspended more than once from teaching (for unknown reasons). However, we find him back at work again in 1711 while preparing the *Estro armonico* for publication. The period after 1712 was a hectic one for Vivaldi the composer, and to this was added the fatigue of continual journeys in Italy and abroad. We find him in Padua, Mantua, Florence and Rome, and even in Amsterdam and Vienna. It is difficult

"Il ritorno del Bucintoro al molo nel giorno dell'Ascensione" (The Return of the Bucentaur to the Pier on Ascension Day). Canaletto.
Correr Museum, Venice.

to see how Vivaldi, a man of uncertain health as he himself always said, could have tolerated the discomfort that long periods away from home inevitably brought in those days, but tolerate it he did, insisting always on personally supervising performances of the many operas he wrote during this period (his catalogue already contained 45 operas – approximately two a year).

His début took place in Vicenza in 1713 with *Ottone in villa*, followed in 1714 by *Orlando finto pazzo* in Venice at the Sant' Angelo, which soon became his favourite theatre. The German aristocrat and amateur musician Johann von Uffenbach, who regularly went to the theatre has left us a diary in which he recorded his impressions of Vivaldi's works. 'The impresario was the famous Vivaldi, who also wrote the opera itself, which was extremely pleasant and charming to watch. The sets and machines were not as costly as in other theatres, and the orchestra was smaller, but it was well worth watching all the same.'

In 1716 Vivaldi mounted three new operas and an oratorio, *Juditha triumphans*, the only one of his three oratorios to have survived. However, he also remained a prolific composer of instrumental music, much of which was published during this period, including *La Stravaganza* Op. 5 (a collection of concertos for violin and strings), Violin Sonatas Op. 5, Concertos for violin and strings Op. 6, Concertos for violin, oboe and strings Op. 7.

Johann Georg Pisendel, a young German violinist in the service of the King of Saxony, was in Venice in 1716 and became Vivaldi's pupil, attracted by his prestige as a composer in the musical life of the city.

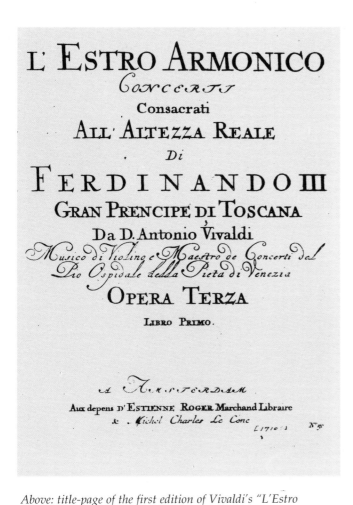

L'ESTRO ARMONICO
Concerti
Consacrati
ALL' ALTEZZA REALE
Di
FERDINANDO III
GRAN PRENCIPE DI TOSCANA
Da D. Antonio Vivaldi
*Musico di Violino e Maestro de Concerti del
Pio Ospidale della Pietà di Venezia*
OPERA TERZA
LIBRO PRIMO.

A AMSTERDAM
Aux depens D'ESTIENNE ROGER Marchand Libraire
& Michel Charles Le Cene   N° 5°

Above: title-page of the first edition of Vivaldi's "L'Estro Armonico", Op. 3, Book 1, published in Amsterdam in 1712. Accademia Musicale Chigiana, Siena.
Below: portrait of Benedetto Marcello. Civica Raccolta di Stampe Bertarelli, Milan. Detail of the title-page of "Il Teatro alla Moda", printed around 1720. Biblioteca Trivulziana, Milan.

He has left us valuable information about Vivaldi's famous improvisations and his extraordinary virtuosity as a violinist. In the meanwhile, Vivaldi continued his work as an opera composer and impresario, which on many occasions took him to places far from Venice. In order to curtail some of their famous teacher's travelling, the Pietà obliged him to give at least two concerts a month with all necessary rehearsals.

His opera *Scanderberg* was performed in Florence in 1718, and in Mantua Vivaldi mounted operas at the Archducal Theatre for Prince Philip of Hesse-Darmstadt, who was vice-regent there. It was probably here that he met a singer, Anna Girì, to whom he soon became attached emotionally as well as artistically – a relationship that created many problems for him. His rate of composition seemed to slacken slightly when a libellous satire entitled ***Fashionable theatre, or a sure and easy way to compose and perform Italian works well...*** was printed and distributed in Venice in 1720. Though anonymous, it soon became known that the author was in fact Benedetto Marcello, and that the satire was directed at the Red Priest. The whole of Venice was privy to the affair, and news of it even reached Vienna. This may be the reason why Vivaldi withdrew from the Venetian scene until 1726. He spent more years working and travelling, and was widely successful. This may have been the happiest and most satisfying period in the whole of his restless composing life.

The vitality and expressive power of his instru-

mental music was totally vindicated by his decision in 1725 to have a new collection of concertos printed by Le Cène in Amsterdam. This new Op. 8 was entitled *Il Cimento dell' armonia e dell' invenzione* (The trial of harmony and invention), in which the

"Cantata delle Putte delli Ospitali nella Procuratia Fila Monici fatta alli Duchi del Norde". 18th-century painting by Gabriele Bella. Pinacoteca Querini Stampalia, Venice.

characteristic descriptive elements in his music reached new heights of brilliance, especially in the group of four concertos called *Le quattro stagioni* (The four seasons), dedicated to the Bohemian Count Venceslao Monzin. The dedication includes: 'I thought it right to publish them, for whatever these concertos might be, with added Sonnets and explanations of all that is written, I feel they will be seen to be quite new'. Thus, Vivaldi himself explains exactly what his descriptive music refers to, perhaps in order to justify the unaccustomed brilliance of the writing. The concertos were well received in France, where the concept of 'imitating nature' was well established and accepted. That Vivaldi was popular in France is further confirmed by the three Serenades he wrote during this period for the French royal family. One of them, *La Senna festeggiante* (The Seine rejoicing), a sumptuous composition very much in the French style of the day, was written in 1720 for Louis XV.

Other works published in Amsterdam between 1727 and 1729 were a collection of Violin Concertos, *La Cetra* (The poet's lyre), Op. 9, in which he returns to his earlier form of solo writing for the instrument, another collection of Flute Concertos, Op. 10, and two other Violin Concertos, Op. 11 and Op. 12. His fame was spreading fast. *The four seasons* was performed in Paris on 7 February 1728, and he met the Emperor Karl VI of Hapsburg in Trieste later that year, dedicating *La Cetra* to him. His fame reached its peak in 1738 when he was invited to Amsterdam for the centenary celebrations of its local opera house. Vivaldi, now in his seventies, had the honour of conducting his *Concerto grosso for ten instruments* (violin, oboe, hunting horns, strings and timpani). He was justly grateful to Holland, for it had been instrumental in getting his music known in Europe, and he knew he was appreciated there. Returning to Venice, he mounted his opera *L'oracolo in Messenia* for the carnival season that year, and after an unsuccessful attempt to mount an opera season in Ferrara, returned to his teaching and

CONCERTI

con molti Istromenti
Suonati dalle Figlie del Pio Ospitale della Pietà
avanti

SUA ALTEZZA REALE
Il Serenissimo

FEDERICO CHRISTIANO
Prencipe Reale di Polonia, et Elettorale di Sassonia.

MUSICA
di D. Antonio Vivaldi
Maestro de Concerti dell'Ospitale sudetto.
In Venezia nell' Anno 1740.

*Title-page of the concertos composed by Vivaldi in honour of
Frederick Christian, Prince of Poland.
Sächsische Landesbibliothek, Dresden.*

*Carnival show in honour of Frederick Christian, Prince of
Poland, in 1740 in the Grimani Theatre, Venice.
Kupfertischkabinett, Dresden.*

playing at the Pietà, where he performed an eclogue, *Il mopso*, in the presence of Ferdinand of Bavaria. Another Pietà concert in 1740 was given before Friedrich Christian, Electoral Prince of Poland, from whom he received honours and gifts. The programme, which included three concertos and a symphony, was Vivaldi's farewell to Venice. On 27 April that year he resigned from the Pietà and left for an unknown destination. His name was gradually forgotten and his music no longer pleased audiences as it once had.

The fame which Vivaldi had won and maintained for the best part of his life vanished during these final years as quickly and as mysteriously as it had come. Even the records of his life tail away and die. What documents we have show that he died a lonely pauper's death in Vienna in the summer of 1741 and was buried in a workhouse cemetery. When the cemetery was later dug up, the unidentified bones of the Red Priest were thrown into a communal grave.

Although many of his contemporaries had imme-

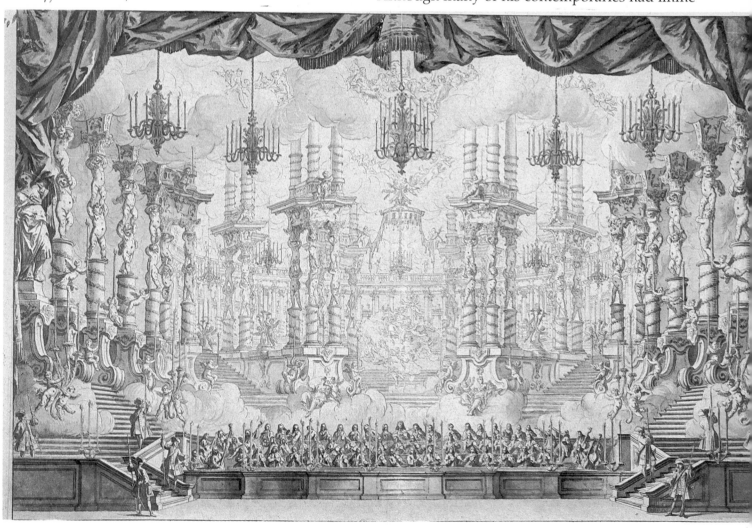

Autograph manuscript of Vivaldi's overture for "Al Santo Sepolcro". Biblioteca Nazionale, Turin.

diately admired his music, Vivaldi had also had his critics. We know that Carlo Goldoni was less than charitable about him, that Tartini did not like his vocal works, and that Benedetto Marcello ridiculed his stylistic tricks. More recently, Stravinsky also was less than kind: 'Vivaldi ... the man who wrote the same concerto six hundred times'.

Vivaldi vanished from musical history and criticism almost immediately after his death, until a search for documentation relating to Bach in 1800 turned up a large bundle of manuscripts dated 1739, bearing both Vivaldi's name and a note in rather poor Italian reading: '... Concertos by Vivaldi written out by J.S. Bach'. This clearly shows that the great German composer knew and admired Vivaldi.

The rediscovery of Vivaldi's music continued into the twentieth century. A huge store of manuscripts was found in Turin in the late 1920s, and this has enabled us to assess the quality of Vivaldi's musical output as a whole. His many works for the Italian theatres of his day testify to his greatness as an opera composer, which was recognised at the time. 'Il Signor Antonio Vivaldi,' wrote Alessandro Mar-

cello, 'the famous violin teacher who is coming to Rome for the carnival Opera.' A document from the Sant' Angelo theatre refers to 'The Reverend Signor Vivaldi who is doing operas in this theatre ...', and in a letter dated 2 January 1739 written by Vivaldi himself, we find: '... anyway, after the ninety-four operas I have composed ...'.

The priest violinist certainly wrote operas, but he was also a highly skilled instrumental composer. As both a performer and a composer he dominated the violin world of eighteenth-century Italy: his masterpieces for the instrument are numerous and of exceptional quality. Many of his concertos glorify the violin as a solo instrument, but he wrote others for a whole variety of solo instruments or groups of instruments. This reflects his long and various experience as a teacher at the Pietà in Venice. His musical palette was broad and colourful, and his concertos range from the daring virtuosity of certain solo works to the dialogues and more intimate singing style of his concertos 'for many instruments'. It is this range of compositions which makes 'The Red Priest' such an important figure in the history of music.

Stage		
46 operas (19 lost)	including:	
	Ottone in villa	1713
	Orlando finto pazzo	1714
	La costanza trionfante degli amore e degli odii	1716
	Scanderberg	1718
	Ercole sul Termodonte	1724
	Il Giustino	1724
	Il Tigrane	1724
	Orlando furioso	1717
	La fida ninfa	1733
	L'Olimpiade	1734
	Griselda	1737
	Catone in Utica	1737
	Tito Manlio	-
3 oratorios	including:	
	Juditha triumphans	-

Vocal		
90 works	including:	
	Beatus vir	-
	Credo	-
	2 Gloria	-
	Kyrie	-
	La Senna festeggiante (serenade)	1720c

Instrumental		
473 concertos for strings & organ/ harpsichord/basso continuo, published in various collections or still in manuscript	13 "symphonies"	-
	187 for violin	-
	6 for viola d'amore	-
	27 for cello	-
	12 for violin and other solo strings	-
	2 for mandolin	-
	16 for flute (or ottavino)	-
	15 for oboe	-
	39 for bassoon	-
	1 for trumpet	-
	2 for horn	-
	102 for solo strings	-
	51 for various groups of soloists	-
72 sonatas for 1 or more instruments and basso continuo	48 for violin (or 2 violins)	-
	4 for winds	-
	4 for various instruments	-
	6 for musette, flute, oboe & violin	-
	9 for cello	-
	1 in trio	-

Händel

Portrait of Händel by Thomas Hudson.

George Frideric Händel, perhaps the most representative of all Baroque composers, was born in Halle on 23 February 1685, the same year in which another great German composer, Johann Sebastian Bach, was born not so very far away. His family was well off, and his father, surgeon to Frederick III of Hohenzollern, the Elector Prince of Brandenburg, wanted him to become a lawyer, but he had a natural talent for music and made rapid progress in his first lessons with Friedrich W. Zachow, organist in the church at Halle. Händel's teacher soon realised that his young pupil was exceptionally gifted and allowed him almost at once to use the organ to compose cantatas for church services.

In addition to his music studies, Händel received a solid general education and was an able student at university. Although he never completed his studies in law, there is little doubt that he was much more highly educated than other musicians of his time.

By 1703 Händel was a violinist in the Gänsemarkt opera house orchestra in Hamburg, where he remained for the next three years, becoming a close friend of the successful opera composer Johann Mattheson who involved him in the theatrical life of the city. At the time, Hamburg was the musical capital of Germany and had the first public opera house in that country, the Gänsemarkt, where German opera was in the process of being born. Eager to learn about operatic and stage technique, Händel remained in his post as violinist, but later won a competition for the post of opera house harpsichordist. His famous journey to Lübeck with his friend Mattheson to visit the great organist Dietrich Buxtehude dates from this period. He heard Buxtehude play in the Marienkirche, tried out organs and harpsichords, and began to think that he might be able take over the old man's post when he retired, but a curious old clause in the contract stipulated that the new incumbent would have to marry the daughter of the present holder of the post. Buxtehude's daughter was not particularly good-looking and Händel was discouraged enough to let pass this important professional opportunity. The young composer began to make a name for himself in Hamburg in 1704 with the composition of his first melodrama, *Almira*, which was followed

The German university of Halle in an 18th-century print. Händelhaus, Halle.

shortly after by *Nero*. Both works were performed early in 1705, *Almira* being reasonably successful, but *Nero* a failure. However, although he now felt ready to become a professional composer, Händel realised that he still lacked first-hand experience and the kind of fluency that all successful opera composers needed; Italy, whose opera composers were most fashionable at the time, was the only place where he could acquire this experience.

The idea that he should leave the Nordic chill of Hamburg for sunnier Italian climes came from an Italian prince, Gian Gastone de' Medici, son of the Grand Duke of Tuscany, who, impressed by Händel's obvious talent, invited him to Florence. And so, having crossed the Alps late in 1706, Händel visited Venice briefly before making his way to Florence, where he played for the Medici court. He did not stay there for very long, however, just enough time to be commissioned to write an opera (*Rodrigo*, 1707-09), and to become the friend of the Grand Duke Cosimo III's youngest son – probably because he loved music much more than his father did (he even had a small private theatre where performances of the most fashionable melodramas of the time were given).

We know from a reliable document in the Capitoline Library that Händel was certainly in Rome on 14 January 1707: "On 14th February there came to this city a Saxon, an excellent harpsichordist and composer, who displayed his talents by playing the organ in the Church of San Giovanni, to the amazement of all who were present".

His name quickly became known throughout the city and leading figures at the Pontifical court vied for the honour of having him in their homes. Händel thus won the friendship and esteem of Cardinals Pamphili, Ottoboni and Colonna. As a result, he managed to have his oratorio *Il trionfo del tempo e del disganno* (The Triumph of Time and Disenchantment) performed in Ottoboni's home with Arcangelo Corelli as conductor, and another oratorio, *La resurrezione*, was performed in the palace of the Marquis Ruspoli in 1708, again under Corelli, with exceptionally large orchestral and choral forces. The whole aristocracy of Rome was present at the Easter Day performance, which was a triumph and immediately became the most talked-of musical event in Rome.

Händel also met many of Italy's leading musicians during his stay in Rome: Arcangelo Corelli, Alessandro and Domenico Scarlatti, and Bernardo Pasquini. He was fascinated by Corelli, whose instru-

18th-century London in a painting by Canaletto. Národní Galerie, Prague.

mental and solo sonatas he was already familiar with, and his later works were profoundly influenced by Corelli's composing style.

Although Rome remained his favourite city, Händel also travelled to other cities for reasons of work. In the summer of 1708 he was in Naples for a performance of his serenade *Acis and Galatea* to celebrate the marriage of the Duke d'Alvito. The following year, on 26 December 1709, he was in Venice for a performance of his second major opera, *Agrippina*, at the San Giovanni Crisostomo opera house. It was another triumph, not least because he enjoyed the protection of Cardinal Grimani who, as well as having written the libretto, actually owned the opera house.

At the height of his popularity, and with *Agrippina* acclaimed as the work of a major new opera composer, Händel decided to leave Italy and return to Germany, having accepted the invitation to become **Kapellmeister** to the Elector Prince of Hannover in 1710. After Italy, Händel was quickly disillusioned with the provincialism of Hannover, and from the beginning regarded his post of **Kapellmeister** as a

stepping stone to greater things. He had set his sights on London, which he dreamed of conquering, especially now that the death of the great English composer Henry Purcell had created a void in the city's musical life in which his own exceptional talent would shine all the more brightly. Having obtained temporary leave from his duties in Hannover, Händel went to London and conducted a triumphant performance of Rinaldo on 24 February 1711. Other opera commissions immediately followed and led to *Il pastor fido* (The faithful shepherd, 1712) and *Teseo* (Theseus, 1713), as well as a number of ceremonial pieces such as the *Ode for the birthday of Queen Anne*, and the *Te Deum* and *Jubilate* written to mark the signing of the Peace of Utrecht.

However, the composer's prolonged absence had incurred the displeasure of the Elector Prince of Hannover who, on the death of Queen Anne, was called upon to take possession of the English throne as George I. Fortunately, their relationship remained cordial enough even after Händel had left the Hannover court for good. He was too proud to be held back by a single patron, however important, and the new English king must have understood this.

Händel's early years in London saw the composition of one of his most famous orchestral works, the *Water music*, which was performed for the first time in the presence of George I on 17 July 1717 by a group of 50 musicians on a boat sailing slowly down the Thames.

In 1717 Händel was invited to join the court of Lord Bridge, Duke of Chandos, at his summer residence, Cannons, and he remained there in the Duke's service for the next two years, composing among other works the *Chandos anthems*, a set of Anglican choral pieces with English texts.

He never lost sight of the theatre, however, producing a revised English version of *Acis and Galatea* (1718) and a biblical drama, *Esther* (1720), again in English. 1719 was an extremely important year in Händel's theatrical career because he was appointed musical director ('Master of Orchestra') at the Haymarket Theatre, where the Royal Academy of Music held its performances, and the King invited him to mount a full-scale opera season there. In order to fulfil his new duties, Händel had to invite prestigious composers and singers over from Germany. The arrival of Giovanni Battista Bononcini in London in 1720 marked the start of an important new phase in its musical life, as well as providing a new creative stimulus for Händel himself. In spite of Bononcini's bitter rivalry and the ridiculous antics of his singers, Händel managed to produce 13 new operas, including *Radamisto* (1720), *Floridante* (1721), *Ottone, Rè di Germania* (Otto, King of Germany) and *Flavio, Rè di Longobardi* (Flavius, King of the Longobards) (both 1723), and two masterpieces, *Giulio Cesare in Egitto* (Julius Caesar in Egypt) and *Tamerlano* (Tamberlaine) (both 1725). These were followed by *Rodelinda* (1725), and *Scipione* and *Alessandro* (1726). He wrote other melodramas, which met with varying success, but important events were now taking place. The Haymarket Theatre was closed, but then reopened under the joint management of Händel and Heidegger, a former impresario, while the supremacy of Italian opera was being challenged by John Gay's English opera *The beggar's opera* with music by Christopher Pepusch.

Händel was not slow in responding. He hired singers in Italy, contacted librettists and composers, and wrote other operas, including *Poro* (1731) and *Orlando* (1733), after a brief period of convalescence following a stroke. His famous early oratorios, *Saul* and *Israel in Egypt*, the opera *Serse*, the six *Concerti Grossi*, Op. 3, the six *Organ Concertos*, Op. 4, the twelve *Concerti Grossi*, Op. 6 and the second set of six *Organ Concertos* (1740) all date from this period. These works are important to our understanding of Händel's musical personality since they are written in a wide range of different forms in which instrumental virtuosity and dialogue assume a new importance.

Title-page of Händel's "Giulio Cesare". Detail. British Museum, London.

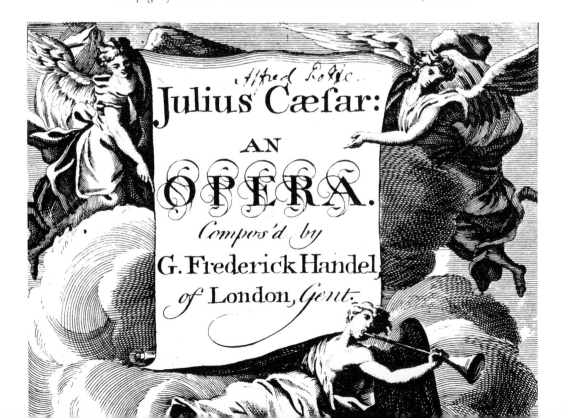

28

"Concert of Songs in Vauxhall Gardens". Tinted print by Robert Pollard, 1786. British Museum, London.

In the meantime, certain aristocratic elements in London opposed to the reigning Hannover dynasty were beginning to object to Händel's presence as a German, even though he had become a naturalised British citizen in 1727. He was forced to hand over the running of the Haymarket Theatre to an Italian consortium led by Porpora, who became the theatre's new manager. Händel moved to the Lincoln Fields Theatre, where he mounted many other operas. His final operas, the unsuccessful *Imeneo* and *Deidamia*, date from 1740-41. The *Messiah* was given its triumphant first performance in Dublin in 1742, where Händel had been invited by the viceroy. He returned to England on 13 August 1742. The oratorio *Samson* was performed early in 1743, and *Judas Maccabeus*, written to support the Hannoverian dynasty against Stuart political aggression, in 1747. The spectacular suite *Music for the royal fireworks* was written in 1749.

Händel suffered a second stroke in 1743 but was soon back at work again, writing a large number of oratorios up to 1750 when he became afflicted with blindness. Revised English versions of several of his works were produced in 1757, and he insisted on being present at a performance of the *Messiah* on 7 April 1759. He died a week later on 14 April 1759 and was buried on the 20th in Westminster Abbey. Händel's works combined the breadth of late German Baroque music with the clarity and charm typical of the English and Italian music of his time, and exerted a powerful influence on English composers for more than a century after his death. The modern revival of his oratorios and theatrical works after a long period of unjustified neglect has restored him to his rightful place among the greatest composers of all time.

Stage

Title	Librettist	Date & place of 1st perf.
Almira	F.C. Feustking (German and English)	8.1.1705 Theater beim Gänsemarkt, Hamburg
Nero (lost)	F.C. Feustking	25.2.1705 Theater beim Gänsemarkt, Hamburg
Florindo e Daphne (lost)	H. Hinsch	January 1708 Theater beim Gänsemarkt, Hamburg
Rodrigo (partially lost)	-	1707-09c Florence
Agrippina	V. Grimani	26.12.1709 Teatro San Giovanni Crisostomo, Venice
Rinaldo (1st version)	G. Rossi	24.2.1711 Queen's Theatre, London
Il Pastor Fido (1st version)	G. Rossi	22.11.1712 Queen's Theatre, London
Ernelinda (pasticcio)	F. Silvani (adapted)	26.2.1713 King's Theatre, London
Teseo	N.F. Haym	10.1.1713 Queen's Theatre, London
Silla	-	1714, London
Amadigi di Gaula	J. Heidegger?	25.5.1715 King's Theatre, London
Acis and Galatea (masque-1st version)	J. Gay & others	1718, Cannons
Radamisto	N.F. Haym	27.4.1720 King's Theatre, London
Haman and Mordecai (masque)	A. Pope and J. Arbuthnot	1720c Cannons
Muzio Scevola (pasticcio)	P.A. Rolli	15.4.1721 King's Theatre, London
Floridante	P.A. Rolli	9.12.1721 King's Theatre, London
Ottone	N.F. Haym	12.1.1723 King's Theatre, London
Flavio	N.F. Haym	14.5.1723 King's Theatre, London
Giulio Cesare	N.F. Haym	20.2.1724 King's Theatre, London
Tamerlano	A. Piovene (adapted N.F. Haym)	31.10.1724 King's Theatre, London
Rodelinda	A. Salvi (adapted N.F. Haym)	13.2.1725 King's Theatre, London
Scipione	P.A. Rolli	12.3.1726 King's Theatre, London
Alessandro	P.A. Rolli	5.5.1726 King's Theatre, London
Admeto	N.F. Haym & P.A. Rolli	31.1.1727 King's Theatre, London
Riccardo Primo	P.A. Rolli	1.11.1727 King's Theatre, London
Siroe	P. Metastasio (reworked by P.A. Rolli or N.F. Haym)	7.2.1728 King's Theatre, London
Poro	P. Metastasio (adapt. S. Humphreys)	2.11.1731 King's Theatre, London
Ezio	P. Metastasio	15.1.1732 King's Theatre, London
Orlando	G. Braccioli	27.1.1733 King's Theatre, London
Il Pastor Fido (3rd vers. with sung ballet Terpsichore)	G. Rossi	9.11.1734 Covent Garden, London
Alcina	A. Marchi	16.4.1735 Covent Garden, London
Atalanta	B. Valeriani (ad.)	12.5.1736 Covent Garden, London
Berenice	A.Salvi	18.5.1737 Covent Garden, London
Faramondo	A. Zeno (with changes)	3.1.1738 King's Theatre, London
Serse	N. Minato (with changes)	15.4.1738 King's Theatre, London
Jupiter in Argos	A.M. Lucchini (ad.)	1.5.1739 King's Theatre, London
Imeneo	-	22.11.1740 Lincoln's Inn Fields Theatre, London
Deidamia	P.A. Rolli	10.1.1741 Lincoln's Inn Fields Theatre, London
Lucio Vero, Imperatore di Rome (pasticcio)	A. Zeno (ad.)	14.11.1747 Lincoln's Inn Fields Theatre, London

Vocal

Sacred

21 oratorios and/or passions	Passion Nach dem Evangelisten Johannes	1704
	Il Trionfo del Tempo e del Disinganno (1737, 1757)	1707
	La Resurrezione	1708
	Esther	1732
	Saul	1739
	Israel in Egypt	1739
	Messiah	1742
	Samson	1743
	Belshazzar	1745
	Judas Maccabeus	1747
	Jephita	1752
approx. 60 sacred works	including:	
	Utrecht Te Deum und Jubilate	1713
	Chandos Anthems (11 pieces)	1717-20c
	Coronation Anthems (4 pieces)	1727
	Deutsche Arien (9 pieces)	1729c
	Dettingen Anthem	1743
	Dettingen Te Deum	1743

Secular

10 various works	Acis and Galatea	1708
	Ode for the Birthday of Queen Anne	1713
	Il Parnaso in Festa	1734
	Ode for St.Cecilia's Day	1739
	Hercules	1745
	The Choice of Hercules	1751
30 cantatas approx.	including:	
	Three English Cantatas	1720-27?c
	Cecilia, volgi uno sguardo	1736

Harpsichord

80 compositions approx.	Suites de Pièces (2 vols)	1723-33
	Six Fugues, Op. 3	?
	Six Easy Fugues (fughettas)	?
	Twelve Fantasias and Four Pieces	?

Chamber

approx. 60 works	including:	
	Six trio sonatas (2 oboes & continuo)	1696c
	Three solo sonatas (flute & continuo)	1730c
	Fifteen solo sonatas (flute, violin, continuo)	1731c
	Seven trio sonatas (2 violins or flute continuo)	1739

Orchestral

19 concerti grossi	Six Concerti Grossi, Op. 3	1734
	Concerto Grosso in C major	1736
	Twelve Concerti Grossi, Op. 6	1740c
10 various concertos		1703-49c
Various works	including:	
	Water Music	1715-17c
	Fireworks Music	1749

Organ

21 concertos	Six Concertos (1st set)	1735-36c
	Six Concertos (2nd set)	1739-40
	Six Concertos (3rd set)	1740-51
	Concerto in D minor for 2 organs	-
	Concerto in D minor	-
	Concerto in F major	1740-50

Songs

approx. 45 arias	including:	
	German Songs (3 pieces)	1696-98c
	French Arias (7 pieces)	1707-09c
	English Minuet Songs (24 pieces)	pub. 1731
21 duets with basso continuo	Italian duets with continuo	1707-45
2 trios with basso continuo	Italian Trios with continuo	1708c
76 cantatas with basso continuo	–	1706-10

Haydn

Portrait of Franz Joseph Haydn. Unknown artist. Civico Museo Bibliografico Musicale, Bologna.

Franz Joseph Haydn was born in Rohrau in Lower Austria into a modest family of craftsmen, on 31 March 1732. There was no musical tradition whatever in the family, but because he had a fine voice he was sent to study with a cousin, Johann Matthias Franck, in Hainburg. His singing ability and exceptional musical ability soon attracted the notice of the composer Georg von Reutter, who was also *Kapellmeister* at St Stephen's Church in Vienna, and Haydn was soon singing soprano parts in his choir there, a post he held for the next 11 years, until his voice broke in 1749.

Haydn acquired wide experience of sacred music during his time with the boys' choir at St Stephen's, but he soon realised that, being only a singer, he would have to study hard under good teachers to make up his lack of theoretical knowledge. He was extremely poor for a number of years, but he studied well and also started composing on commission. Only a Missa brevis in F major (1749-50) has survived from this period, probably composed shortly after another Mass and a *Salve regina* for soprano, chorus and strings.

In 1751 Haydn attracted notice with a *Singspiel*, *Der krumme Teufel*, with a libretto by Joseph F. Kurz based on Lesage's *Le diable boiteux*. This brilliant

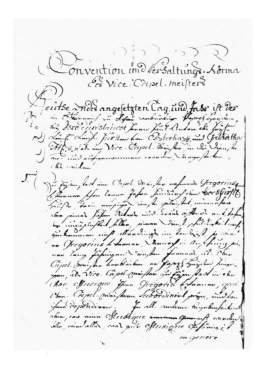

Page of the contract confirming Haydn's appointment in 1761 as deputy Kapellmeister to the Esterházy Princes. Széchényi National Library, Budapest.

piece packed with comic scenes gave Haydn valuable experience in *opera buffa* composition, although the genre was never particularly congenial to him. He was living at that time in the attic of the house in which the Italian court poet Pietro Metastasio also lived on the first floor. This proved extremely useful, for Metastasio recommended him as harpsichord teacher to Maria Anna Martinez, the young daughter of a functionary at the Apostolic Nunciary. The next few years were profitable and enjoyable for Haydn because he was able to meet important musical figures of his day in the home of his wealthy patron. He saw Porpora, his young pupil's singing teacher, virtually every day, and met Gluck and Karl Ditters von Dittersdorf, the composer and

The actual visiting card Haydn had printed towards the end of his life. In addition to his name, a brief snatch of melody appears beside the motto "All my strength has gone ..."

violinist. He was also introduced to Wagenseil, harpsichord teacher to Maria Theresia of Austria. The young Haydn was obliged to familiarise himself with a variety of musical styles and schools, ranging from Italian *opera seria* to the German symphonic school. A symphony, a number of divertimenti for various instruments, and his first Harpsichord Sonata date from this period. His first six String Quartets, Op. 1, were composed between 1755 and 1760. These early quartets contain all the elements of Haydn's characteristic style, and he was instrumental in establishing the string quartet as a genre in its own right.

In 1759 Haydn obtained the important post of *Musikdirektor* and *Kammercomponist* (music director and chamber composer) to Count Ferdinand Maximilian Morzin, which meant spending part of his time in Vienna and the rest at the Count's coun-

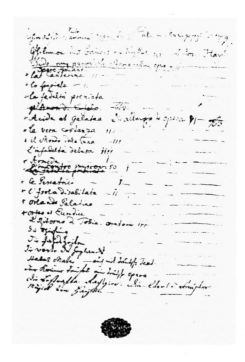

Autograph list of Haydn's works. Historisches Museum der Stadt, Vienna.

try residence in Bohemia, where a small, 15-piece orchestra of strings and flutes had been formed. Haydn's Symphony No. 1, and probably also Symphonies No. 2 and 5, were written for this orchestra. He held the post for only two years, however, when the Count was oblige to disband the orchestra for financial reasons. The composer's life had now reached a turning point. Still only in his late twenties, he signed a contract to work for Prince Paul Anton Esterházy on 1 May 1761. Less wisely, he also contracted an unsuccessful marriage.

The powerful Esterházy princes, closely connected to the imperial Hapsburg family, were wealthy Hungarian noblemen whose palace at Eisenstadt was a true court that even had its own small army. When Prince Paul Anton died in 1762, power passed to his brother Nikolaus, nicknamed 'The Magnificent' on account of his grandiose ideas.

Haydn was already installed as *vice-Kapellmeister* at Eisenstadt when this change took place, and had won the esteem of everyone in the orchestra there, although the old *Kapellmeister*, Werner, remained somewhat hostile towards him. Relations with the new Prince were not always ideal, but he had a real passion for music and this enabled Haydn to gain wide experience as composer and conductor because he was at last free from financial worry. The Prince loved to play the 'barytone', a sort of viola da gamba fashionable at the time, and

not surprisingly, Haydn wrote 126 trios and 25 duets for barytone and strings – typical examples of pieces written on commission to suit the musical taste and ability of the person who had to play them.

Other more important compositions of this period include three named symphonies, No. 6 ('*Le matin*'), No. 7 ('*Le midi*') and No. 8 ('*Le soir*'), as well as symphonies Nos. 13, 22 ('*Der Philosoph*'), 31 and 40. All these works were written for strings, basso continuo and a handful of wind instruments. Some of the concertos of this period were written to display the technical skills of the players Haydn had available at any given moment, or for Prince Nikolaus' own daily musical performances. It seems that Haydn composed at least a hundred trios for the Prince during his time at Eisenstadt.

In 1766, the Prince moved his residence from Eisen-

An opera performance in Prince Esterházy's theatre with Haydn conducting the orchestra from the harpsichord.
Tempera. Österreichische Nationalbibliothek, Vienna.

stadt to Esterhaz where a new palace with a theatre, church and magnificent park had been specially built. In view of the grandeur of his establishment, Nikolaus decided to augment his orchestra to 20 players with the addition of trumpets, flutes, a bassoon and timpani. Haydn came into his own in the new residence at Esterhaz. Having been appointed *Kapellmeister* after the death of Werner, the previous incumbent, he was now responsible for all music played at court. The quality and quantity of his output during the 30 years he spent at Esterhaz is extraordinary, and in addition to his composing, he mounted several hundred performances of Italian operas and himself wrote eleven melodramas (one, *The uninhabited island*, has a libretto by Metastasio) and five operas for the puppet theatre there. Although his output of sacred music was much less abundant (it included only

Beethoven compliments Haydn after a performance of "The Creation" on 27 March 1808 in Vienna. Print from a watercolour. Österreichische Nationalbibliothek, Vienna.

Oil portrait of Joseph Haydn by Thomas Hardy, London 1791. Royal College of Music, London.

the *Missa Sancta Caeciliae*, the *Missa Collensis* and the *Stabat Mater*), the symphony and string quartet remained central to his work as a composer. Of the many symphonies written at Esterhaz, perhaps the most famous are No. 44 (*Trauersymphonie*, or *Funeral Symphony*), No. 45 (*Farewell*), No. 49 (*The Passion*) and No. 73 (*The Hunt*). Haydn's music was now known throughout Europe, and his reputation was confirmed when his works began to be played regularly in Paris, Amsterdam, Vienna and Berlin.

When the orchestra was disbanded after the death of Prince Nikolaus in 1790, Haydn had no difficulty in finding a new post. The German violinist and impresario Johann Peter Salomon, who had settled in London many years before, quickly persuaded Haydn to join him there. During his relatively short first stay in London (January 1791 to June 1792) Haydn conducted many of Salomon's concerts, was presented at court, heard Händel's oratorios and was awarded an honorary doctorate of music by Oxford University. He revised the existing Sym-

phony No. 92 specially for this occasion, and it soon came to be known as the *Oxford Symphony*. It was performed in a concert of his works which included the madrigal for chorus and orchestra (*The Tempest*), Symphonies Nos. 93 and 98, and the *Sinfonia concertante* for oboe, bassoon, violin, cello and orchestra.

Leaving London in mid 1792, Haydn returned to Vienna via Bonn. There he met and encouraged the young Ludwig van Beethoven who later followed him to Vienna. However, Haydn himself did not stay there very long. After writing the String Quartets, Opp. 71 and 74, the Variations in F minor for keyboard, a symphony and a number of pieces for mechanical instruments, he returned to London in 1794, where he remained until August 1795, repeating the success of his previous visit. His symphonies were again much played: Nos. 99 and 104 (*Salomon*) are perhaps the greatest he ever wrote, and the so-called 'London Symphonies' (Nos. 93-104) were given popular names by which they are most often known today (No. 94, *Surprise*; No. 96,

Title-page of Haydn's "The Four Seasons"
Österreichische Nationalbibliothek, Vienna.

Silhouette of Haydn.

Ticket for a performance of Haydn's "The Four Seasons". Engraving by J. Berka. Österreichische Nationalbibliothek, Vienna.

Miracle; No. 100, *Military*; No. 101, *Clock*; No. 102, *Drum Roll*; No. 104, *Salomon*). He also experimented further with the form of the trio and the sonata during his stay in London, producing the remarkable Trios Nos. 26 and 30, and Sonatas Nos. 50 and 52. Returning definitively to Vienna in mid 1795, Haydn resumed his post as director of music to the Esterházy family (the court **Kapell** having been re-established by Nikolaus II during his absence), but he spent most of his time in Vienna composing such works as the famous String Quartets, Op. 76 (the third of which is the famous *Emperor Quartet*), the three String Quartets, Op. 77, and the *Trumpet Concerto*. However, sacred music dominated the output of his final years: six great Masses for soloists, chorus and orchestra, and two great Oratorios, *The Creation* (1798) and *The seasons* (1801). One string quartet, begun in 1803 when Haydn was old and tired, remained unfinished.

He was made an honorary citizen of Vienna in 1804, and was present at a performance of *The Creation* conducted by Salieri in 1808. 'The father of the symphony' died peacefully in Vienna on 31 May 1809.

The symphony was still a very young genre when Haydn began to compose for it in 1759 (five or six years before Mozart). It was basically a three-movement instrumental piece that had grown out of the orchestral introductions or overtures to operas (in fact, overtures are still called *sinfonie* (symphonies) in Italian). These early symphonies were played at the beginning and end of concerts whose main attractions were soloists, singers or instrumental groups.

The Italian symphonic format was soon modified in Germany because orchestras there were larger and technically more accomplished, which meant that they could produce much more sound. German composers had, in effect, a different concept of orchestral sound, and the symphonies they composed became more complex and more varied thematically. The forms of the existing three movements were expanded and developed, and a fourth movement, a minuet or scherzo, was added. Gradually, the orchestral symphony undermined the supremacy of works for singers to become the main feature of concerts, as was the case with Haydn's last symphonies, Mozart's symphonies after 1786, and all Beethoven's symphonies.

Haydn also wrote masterly string quartets, and was instrumental in establishing the quartet as an important genre in its own right. His international fame as a quartet composer equalled that of Boccherini in his own lifetime. Haydn's 82 string quartets are still a serious challenge for all professional quartet players as well as composers on account of his extensive use of contrapuntal writing. After Haydn, Mozart and Beethoven (whom he admired) raised these forms to even greater heights.

The entrance to the Augarten in Vienna. 18th-century print. Albertina Graphische Sammlungen, Vienna.

Stage

23 operas	including:	
	Lo speziale	1768
	L'incontro improvviso (The Unexpected Meeting)	1775
	Il mondo della luna (The World of the Moon)	1777
	Orlando paladino (Orlando the Paladin)	1782
	Orfeo ed Euride, or L'anima del filosofo	1791
	(Orpheus & Eurydice, or The Philosopher's Soul)	

Vocal

Sacred

14 masses	Missa brevis	1749-50
	Missa solemnis (Grosse Orgelmesse)	1766
	Missa Sancta Caeciliae	1769-73
	Missa Cellensis (Mariazellermesse)	1782
	Missa Sancti Bernardi de Offida	
	(Heiligenmesse)	1796
	Missa in angustiis (Nelson Mass)	1798
	Theresien-Messe	1799
	Missa solemnis (Schöpfungs-Messe)	1801
	Missa (Harmoniemesse)	1802
5 oratorios including:	Il ritorno di Tobia (Tobia's Return)	1774-75
	The Creation	1798
	The Seasons	1801
14 other works	including:	
	2 Salve regina	1756-71
	2 Te Deum	1764c-1800
	1 Stabat Mater	1773c
10 canons	Die heiligen zehn Gebote	1791-95

Secular

13 choral cantatas	including:	
	Esterhazy Festkantate	1763-64
	The Tempest	1791-92
4 solo cantatas		1782-89
1 terzetto	Pietà di me, benigni dèi	-
4 duets		1794-96
approx. 30 arias		1787-90
46 canons		1790-1800

Orchestral

108 symphonies	including:	
	D major ('Le matin')	1761
	C major ('Le midi')	1761
	G major ('Le soir' or 'The Tempest')	1761
	E flat major ('The Philosopher')	1764
	F minor ('La passione')	1768
	A major ('Fire')	1769c
	E minor ('Funeral')	1771c
	F sharp minor ('Farewell')	1772
	C major ('Maria Theresia')	1772-73
	C major ('Il distratto')	1774-75
	C major ('La Roxelane')	1777
	D major ('The Hunt')	1781
	G minor ('The Hen')	1785
	C major ('The Bear')	1786
	B flat major ('The Queen')	1785-86
	G major ('Oxford')	1788?
	G major ('Surprise')	1791
	G major ('Military')	1794
	E flat major ('Drumroll')	1795
	D major ('Salomon')	1795
16 overtures		1762-80
8 marches		1792-95
dances (single or sets)	including:	
	approx. 200 minuets	1760-92
	approx. 60 German dances	1787?
also	The Seven Last Words	1785

Concertos

32 concertos for 1 or more instruments	11 for piano	1756-82c
	4 for violin	1756-70c
	5 for cello	1769c-83
	1 for double bass	?
	1 for flute	1780c
	1 for two horns	?
	3 for horn	1762-65c
	5 for two harps	1786
	1 for trumpet	1796

Chamber

83 string quartets	Op. 1	1755-60
	Op. 2	1760c
	Op. 3	1763-65?
	Op. 9	1769c
	Op. 17	1771
	Op. 20 ('Sun' Quartets)	1772
	Op. 33 ('Russian' Quartets)	1778-81
	Op. 42	1785
	Op. 50 ('Prussian' Quartets)	1787
	Op. 51 ('The Seven Last Words')	1787
	Op. 54	1788?
	Op. 55	1788?
	Op. 64	1790
	Op. 71 ('Apponyi' Quartets)	1793
	Op. 74 ('Apponyi' Quartets)	1793
	Op. 76 ('Erdödy' Quartets)	1797-99
	Op. 77 ('Lobkowitz' Quartets)	1799
	Op. 103 (unfinished)	1803
188 trios	41 for piano (harpsichord), violin (flute) and cello	1766-97
	21 for 2 violins and cello	1767-68
	126 for two barytons (violins) and cello	1767-75
31 duets	25 for baryton and cello	1765-70
	6 for violin and viola	1799
87 divertimenti	51 for 4 or more parts (various instr.)	1754-90
	11 for three parts (various instr.)	1767-94
	12 for baryton and instruments	1767-75
	13 with harpsichord	1764-69
also	32 pieces for flute-clock	1772-93

Songs

48 songs (approx. 4 sets & approx. 12 individual)	including:	
	XII Lieder für Clavier. Erster Teil	1781
	XII Lieder für Clavier. Zweiter Teil	1784
	VI Original Canzonettas. First Set	1794
	VI Original Canzonettas. Second Set	1795
also	13 vocal trios and/or quartets with piano	1796c
	approx. 400 arrangements of popular songs	1792-1839
		(post.)

Piano

52 sonatas and/or divertimenti	including:	
	D major (Divertimenta ac Galantheriae)	1767
	Six sonatas	1771-80?
	Six sonatas	1773
	Six sonatas	1774-76
	Three sonatas	1784
	Three divertimenti	1765-67?
12 various pieces	including:	
	Capriccio	1765
	5 Variations	1766c
	Fantasia	1789
also	2 pieces for piano duet	1778c

Mozart

AMEDEO VOLFANGO MOZARTO SALISBVRGENSI
PVERO DVODENNI
IN ARTE MVSICA LAVDEM OMNEM FIDEMQ. PRAETERGRESSO
EOQ. NOMINE GALLORVM ANGLORVMQ. REGIBVS CARO
PETRVS LVIATVS HOSPITI SVAVISSIMO
EFFIGIEM IN DOMESTICO ODEO P. C.
ANNO CIƆIƆCCLXX.

View of Salzburg in a tinted engraving. Albertina Graphische Sammlungen, Vienna.

Page 39: Portrait of Wolfgang Amadeus Mozart painted by Saverio della Rosa in Verona, 1770. Museo Civico, Verona.

When Wolfgang Amadeus Mozart was born in Salzburg on 27 January 1756, his family was enjoying a period of relative prosperity. His father Leopold, a respected violinist, worked in the Chapel of the Archbishop of Salzburg and was able to offer a secure future to Maria Anna and Wolfgang, the only two surviving children of the six his wife Anna Maria had borne him.

Most important of all, he was able to offer them a happy home and the abundant affection that Wolfgang immediately showed he needed. A quiet though by no means shy child, Wolfgang revealed an innate talent for music at an extremely early age, which his father quickly developed through strict discipline and study as soon as he became aware of it. He taught his son the violin and the piano, played a key role in his first attempts at composition, and presented him in the salons of the nobility where he was fêted by aristocratic ladies amazed by his prodigious talent. Fortunately, such early public exposure did not warp the personality of the little boy; he managed to preserve his natural innocence and charm.

Leopold's travels with his two small children began very early. By 1762, when Wolfgang was barely six, the Mozarts were already journeying around Europe. Wolfgang's sister Maria Anna, whom he affectionately called Nannerl, was herself an excellent pianist. They played together several times in Munich during carnival time before the Electoral Prince Maximillian, and were very well received. The Mozart family moved to Vienna in September 1762. We know from some of Leopold's letters that the Empress Maria Theresia invited the musical family to Schönbrunn even before they had requested an audience.

In June 1763 the family set off from Salzburg on a much longer tour that would last about three years. Having returned to Munich, where they were received at court, they moved on to Augsburg where they aroused considerably less interest. In Frankfurt, however, the five public concerts of the two young musicians attracted huge audiences. After Germany, the family moved on to Brussels and then, in April 1764, London. The triumph of Wolfgang's audience with George III equalled the sensation he had caused in Paris a few months before. In London, the young Mozart was able to meet Johann Christian Bach, son of Johann Sebastian, and hear his music. They became close friends, and Johann Christian's music had an important influence on Wolfgang's own compositions. He was already writing symphonies and sonatas for violin and piano, and these were soon followed by his first operas, *La finta semplice* (1768), an *opera buffa*, and in the same year, the *Singspiel Bastien und Bastienne*.

After a short rest they embarked on their travels once again, this time to Italy. 'My heart overflows with joy,' wrote Mozart on 13 December 1769, the day he set off for the south, 'this journey really is fun.' Having crossed the Brenner Pass into Italy, and after a short stay in Rovereto and a triumphant concert at the Accademia Filharmonica in Verona, Wolfgang and his father made for Milan where they met, among other celebrities, one of the most

Portrait of Leopold Mozart, father of Wolfgang Amadeus. Mozarthaus, Augusta.

Family tree of the Mozart family. Mozarthaus, Augusta.

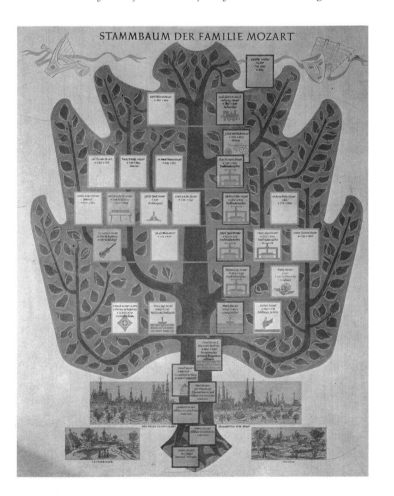

famous musicians of the day, Giovanni Battista Sammartini. Mozart's first String Quartet, dated Lodi 15 March 1770, was written during this period.

Other Italian cities followed – Bologna, Florence, Rome and Naples. In Bologna, he received important tuition from Padre Martini, and on reaching Rome he was awarded The Order of the Golden Spur by Pope Clement XIV.

Returning to the north, Mozart gave a performance of a hastily composed opera, *Mitridate, rè di Ponto*, at the Teatro Ducale in Milan on 26 December 1770. Although by no means a masterpiece, the opera is a fully fledged work in the Italian tradition, and Mozart, it should be remembered, was only 14 at the time.

The Mozart family returned to Salzburg, but not for long; by mid 1771 they were back in Italy again. Wolfgang's opera, *Ascanio in Alba*, was performed on 17 October at the Teatro Ducale in Milan, followed by *Lucio Silla* on 26 December 1772, again at the Teatro Ducale. The success of this opera set the seal on his triumphal third visit to Italy.

Leopold's and Wolfgang's patron, the Archbishop Sigismund, died in December 1771 just after they had returned to Austria, and his successor brought changes to the life they had led up to then. The new Archbishop Hieronymus, Count Colloredo, was less tolerant of the absences of his employees than his predecessor had been, and was less inclined to

The infant Mozart plays the harpsichord accompanied by his father Leopold and his sister Nannerl. Watercolour by L. Carrogis de Carmontelle. Musée Carnavalet, Paris.

grant the Mozart family the long periods of leave they needed for their musical careers. However, Wolfgang composed an allegorical opera, *Il sogno di Scipione* (Scipio's dream) in honour of the new archbishop's enthronement, and the archbishop rewarded Mozart by appointing him *Konzertmeister*, or principal violinist, in Salzburg, a post he held for virtually the next five years. Nonetheless, he was granted leave to make a number of short journeys, and in 1773 went to Vienna with his father. After resigning from the Archbishop's service in September 1777, he went to Augsburg and Mannheim, and in 1778 to Paris, where he felt a free artist for the first time in his life.

However, his success was neither universal nor great. These were difficult years for the young composer and performer. In 1775 he had had *La finta giardiniera* successfully performed in Munich and, shortly afterwards, *Il re pastore*, with a libretto by Pietro Metastasio, at the court of the Archbishop of Salzburg. In Paris, the 22-year-old composer was commissioned in 1778 to write music for the ballet

Les petits riens, but further success eluded him, and to make matters worse, his beloved mother died. He returned to Salzburg in mid January 1779, a desperate and disappointed though rather more mature man, conscious of his real worth and incalculably richer in emotional and intellectual resources.

A glimmer of hope appeared in October 1780 when Mozart, now in the service of the Count Colloredo once more, was commissioned to write a carnival opera for Munich, and the outcome, *Idomeneo*, was performed on 29 January 1781 at the Court Theatre in Munich. The 'new and unusual' work, as it was described, was a great success. Mozart, wishing to savour a little longer the triumph of his work and the public admiration it was winning him, did not return immediately to Salzburg, to the irritation of the Archbishop. This unsatisfactory state of affairs was finally resolved on 16 March 1781, when Mozart left the Archbishop's service for good. From that moment on, the composer was released not only from a commitment he had always found oppres-

The infant Mozart seated next to his father and the Archbishop Prince of Salzburg during a concert. Painting.

sive, but also from the smothering protectiveness of his father. He left Salzburg and plunged at once into the hectic life of Vienna, where he thought he would easily find work as a 'freelance'. Hoping that he would have many pupils, he composed a large number of pedagogical works, feeling confident that he would be commissioned to write at least one opera a year, as well as asked to give many subscription concerts. He was sure, also, that he would have no trouble in getting his compositions published. At first everything seemed to go well, but 1786 was to mark the start of his decline.

He wrote no fewer than 17 concertos between 1782 and 1786, high-spirited concert pieces such as the Concert Rondos in D (K. 382) and A (K. 386), and other more substantial pieces such as symphonies. His next opera, *Die Entführung aus dem Serail* (The abduction from the seraglio) was a triumphant success with the Viennese public when first performed on 16 July 1782 at the Burgtheater, but he never completed his next stage work, the *opera buffa*, *Lo sposo deluso*, begun the following year.

The success of the *Seraglio* was very reassuring for Mozart. He quickly married Constanze Weber on 4 August 1782, heedless of his father's stern disapproval. However, he had plenty of work, and when his father came to visit the new couple in Vienna in

The diploma Mozart received from the Accademia Filharmonica, Bologna. Mozartmuseum der Internationalen Sfiftung Mozarteum, Salzburg.

the winter of 1785, he could only feel reassured by the progress his son seemed to be making. Wolfgang's work was being published, and he had many pupils.

However, this good fortune was to prove short-lived. 1786 saw the first performances of *Le nozze di Figaro*, an opera with a libretto by Lorenzo da Ponte, at the Hoftheater in Vienna. The opera was fairly successful, but the Viennese aristocracy was at a loss to understand the subject of the work. Artists were still looked upon as servants who were not supposed to go beyond certain limits in what they did. By setting the words of a common man, Figaro, to fine music, Mozart was in effect challenging the society of his day. In a sense, then, this opera marked the start of his decline in popularity in Vienna.

Le nozze met with a very different reception at the National Theatre in Prague, however, where the German-Czech aristocracy was in the grip of nationalistic fervour. The triumph of *Le nozze* was equalled by that of his next opera, *Don Giovanni*, first performed on 29 October 1787. The months Mozart spent in Prague were perhaps the happiest of his entire life, and the public esteem he enjoyed compensated him for the bitter disappointments he had known earlier in his career. Matters ended there, however, and he was forced to return to Vienna in search of work.

*An unusual automaton made in 1700. It is, in fact, a wall clock.
Musée des Arts Décoratifs, Paris.*

1788 saw the composition of the Piano Concerto in D major (K. 537). It was performed much later in Frankfurt on 15 October 1790 to mark the crowning of Leopold II, and is, in fact, known as the **Coronation Concerto**.

His last Piano Concerto in B flat major, K. 595, was written early in 1791 and is famous for the feeling of classical repose it shares with all the works Mozart composed in this last year of his life.

The symphonies composed during these final years are also extremely interesting. While preparing to go to Prague for *Le nozze* in December 1786, Mozart wrote his monumental Symphony No.38 in D minor, K. 504, often called the *Prague* or *Sinfonia senza minuetto* (Symphony without a minuet). It was followed in 1788 by Symphony No.39 in E flat major, K. 543, Symphony No.40 in G minor, K. 550, and finally, Symphony No.41 in C major, K. 551, the *Jupiter*.

1789 was perhaps Mozart's most difficult year. In fact, his financial situation was so disastrous that he was desperately searching for the wherewithal simply to live. Things seemed to take a slight turn for the better towards the end of the year when he left for Berlin, hoping to find employment with the Emperor Wilhelm Friedrich II, but the work offered turned out to be a commission for six Quartets and six easy Sonatas for piano, which he never even completed. He also visited Dresden, Leipzig and

View of Vienna. Print. Historisches Museum der Stadt, Vienna.

Prague but received no commissions that might have helped him with his desperate financial situation.

After returning to Vienna in 1789, he presented to the Emperor Joseph II a new *opera buffa*, *Così fan tutte*, again with a libretto by Lorenzo da Ponte. It was performed on 26 January 1789 at the Burgtheater, but the death of the Emperor shortly afterwards on 20 February, put a temporary stop to theatre activity in Vienna, which effectively (though unintentionally) killed Mozart's masterpiece at birth. The opera had been well received, but was not performed again in Vienna for many years.

Another important opportunity seemed to present itself late in 1790, when the impresario Salomon, who was passing through Vienna at the time, offered Mozart a contract for six months' residence in London and also a series of six paid public concerts in Amsterdam. However, the invitations coincided with the start of Mozart's decline in health.

Prague, too, asked Mozart to compose a serious opera to celebrate the coronation of Leopold II as King of Bohemia. The result, *La clemenza di Tito*, composed in just four weeks, was performed in Prague on 6 September 1791 and failed to win the approval of the court, although later performances were popular successes.

Mozart returned to Vienna to assist with rehearsals for another opera he had been working on over previous months, *Il flauto magico* (The magic flute), a musical fantasy based on the poetry of Wieland with a libretto by the impresario E.J. Schikaneder. The premiere on 30 September 1791 at the Theater auf der Wieden in Vienna was by no means a triumph, but *The magic flute* quickly became his most successful opera.

Mozart was now nearing the end of his life. His pallid face and general listlessness already indicated the inevitable approach of death. He himself was aware of this. 'I continue to compose,' he wrote on 7 September 1791, 'because it tires me less than resting does ... I feel that my hour is close at hand; I am near to death ... But life has been so wonderful.' Mozart died in Vienna on 5 October in the same year, perhaps of a kidney infection. He was buried in a communal grave, and his remains have never since been found.

'I continue to compose,' he had said in his last year

of life, and that is exactly what he did. In spite of the weariness it cost him, he never lost the urge to write music. In a letter written by his sister-in-law, Sophie Weber, dated 1825, we read: '... Süssmayr was at Mozart's side. The *Requiem* was spread out on the bed-covers and Mozart was explaining to him how he should finish writing the finale after his death ...' The *Requiem* is Mozart's last great work and one of the greatest pieces of sacred music ever written. An aura of mystery surrounds its birth since it was commissioned by an anonymous benefactor who did not wish to reveal his name. Mozart accepted the commission in return for 50 ducats. However, its composition cost him much anguish, and he died without discovering the identity of his benefactor.

We now know that this mysterious individual was, in fact, Count Franz von Walsegg, whose vanity made him buy up unpublished works in order to pass them off as his own compositions. Later, on 14 December 1793, this strange man conducted the first performance of Mozart's *Requiem* under the vaulted roof of the Wiener Neustadt Cistercian church in Vienna, having first written 'composed by Count Walsegg' on the cover of the score.

Mozart never finished writing his *Requiem*. It was completed by his pupil Franz Xavier Süssmayr, who with humility and skill supplied the missing parts and revised much of the existing manuscript. His revisions seem faithful on the whole to Mo-

Title-page of the Artaria edition (1785) of Mozart's Piano Concerto K.415. Mozartmuseum der Internationalen Sfiftung Mozarteum, Salzburg.

zart's intentions, perhaps because Süssmayr had been very close to his teacher during the last days of his life.

Apart from the *Requiem*, Mozart wrote a large number of other sacred pieces, virtually all of them during his period of service in Salzburg. They include some 15 Masses, Litanies, Vespers and Offertories. As the reduction in his output of religious music from 1785 continued over the next few years, Mozart concentrated increasingly on Masonic music, almost as if the religious impulses he had never been able fully to express in sacred music had been redirected into this new channel. Mozart had become a Mason in 1784. At first, he took little interest in their meetings, but as the public became indifferent to his work, he found the financial assistance the Masons could offer him increasingly useful. His compositions during this period include the cantata *Dir, Seele des Weltalls* (K. 429), performed when Mozart was elected a Mason, the cantata *Die Maurerfreude* (K. 471) performed on 24 April 1785, the cantata *Maurerische Trauermusik* (K. 477), performed on 17 November 1785, and his last finished composition, the short *Masonic Cantata* (K. 623), which he finished in November 1791.

His short Motet in D major *Ave verum corpus*, K. 618, deserves special mention. This masterpiece, dating from the summer of 1791 just before he began the *Requiem*, was composed extremely quickly in response to a commission for a piece for the Feast of Corpus Christi in the church of St Stephen at Baden. Although it has only 46 bars, this tiny motet

Title-page of the complete works of Mozart published in Leipzig. Biblioteca del Conservatorio G. Verdi, Milan.

The singer Oscar Laske as Papageno in Mozart's "The Magic Flute".
Mozartmuseum der Internationalen Sfiftung Mozarteum, Salzburg.

combines stateliness with extraordinary simplicity, and is perhaps the highest expression of the miraculous 'simplicity' Mozart's work embodies to a unique degree.

His output of chamber music was enormous, almost all of it commissioned by bourgeois or noble patrons. It includes divertimenti, serenades, nocturnes and dances for the carnival masked balls that were fashionable at the time. One famous example is his Serenade in G major, *Eine kleine Nachtmusik* (A little night-music) in G major for strings, K. 525, completed on 19 August 1787, a brilliant piece of rather affected charm that intentionally borders on the superficial. The well known divertimento *Ein Musikalischer Spass* (A musical

joke), K. 522, was composed shortly before the Serenade, perhaps his most famous piece.

During the same period he also completed a large number of *Lieder* for voice and piano, including *Abendempfindung*, K. 523, *An Cloe*, K. 524 and *Das Veilchen* (The Violet), K. 476 based on verses by Goethe. This last song is important because it departs from the accepted norms of eighteenth-century vocal music. Mozart derived his new idiom from the dramatic music of his time and added a new expressive dimension to the *Lied* which was to be taken up by Franz Schubert in the following century.

Many other *Lieder* were composed after Mozart's appointment as 'court composer' in Vienna (a high-sounding title which really meant that he had to write a certain number of dances each year for court balls and functions). In addition to the six famous String Quartets dedicated to Haydn, and others written for Frederick Wilhelm of Prussia, his greatest chamber music includes the String Quintet in G minor of 1787, and the Clarinet Quintet of 1789, whose radiant beauty is matched by the Clarinet Concerto in A major, K. 622, of 1791. Nor should his Sonatas for violin and piano be forgotten, wonderful examples of sonatas for one of the most demanding instrumental combinations. Mozart's enormous output also includes works composed in periods of especially acute poverty, which succeed in reconciling an essential frivolity of purpose with an extraordinary originality of concept. Thus, the great Mozart was capable of writing music for the mechanical organs that were built into clocks, like the great Fantasia in F minor, K. 608, composed on 3 March 1790, or the Andante, K. 616, written on 4 May of the same year. There is also music for the glass harmonica, an instrument consisting of glasses tuned at various pitches which 'sing' when the player rubs his moist finger tips around their rims. His *Adagio and Rondo*, K. 617, is a masterpiece for this instrument, or 'medium'. And yet, when the burden of his poverty lifted, even briefly, his greatness reasserted itself to the full and, in the final period of his life, attained its most sublime expression in great vocal works such as *Le nozze di Figaro* (1786), *Don Giovanni* (1790), and *The magic flute* (1791, the year in which he died). Apart from the *Requiem*, his music is essentially happy and seems in no way to foreshadow his death, except perhaps in the indirect sense that death brings release from the cares of human existence.

The first complete edition of Mozart's works, based on the chronological catalogue compiled in 1862 by the musicologist Ludwig Köchel (whose name is represented by the 'K' preceding the numbering of the works), was printed in Leipzig between 1877 and 1905.

Above: Emanuel Schikaneder and the Auf der Wieden theatre as shown in the 1791 "Theatre Almanac".
Österreichische Nationalbibliothek, Vienna.
Below: silhouettes of the leading characters in Mozart's "Don Giovanni" when it was performed in Prague.
Österreichische Nationalbibliothek, Vienna.

The origins of Mozart's style

If we happen to hear a less well known Mozart work without knowing its title, or even that it is by Mozart, we say unhesitatingly that 'this is Mozart' and that 'this is his style'. And yet, we might well be wrong, because Mozart's style was characteristic not only of himself but also of all the composers who wrote in the second half of the eighteenth century.

The essential point is that this style was, as it were, a geographical phenomenon, a cosmopolitan style found throughout musically educated Europe (Italy, Germany, France and some parts of Great Britain). Second, and in a more formal sense, the common musical denominator of the time was the ubiquitous presence of Italian opera, fêted in opera houses throughout Europe.

The key to opera seria was song itself, that is a melody that had to satisfy simultaneously a number of complex requirements. Song alone had to carry virtually all the expressive content of the music, given that the orchestra had an essentially accompanying role, so it had to be able to express a range of basic human emotions (tenderness, joy, pain, exuberance) in the most direct way possible using repeatable, recognisable musical formulas. Moreover, the song's me-

ries (Corelli, Albinoni, Vivaldi, Geminiani, Torelli). Italy's great instrumental composers gradually moved abroad, usually to become teachers, and often abandoned instrumental composition in favour of opera, (as in the case with Jommelli, Traetta, Piccinni and Paesiello), bringing to it the style of the violin compositions they had written earlier in their careers.

German composers had, naturally, had greater difficulty in composing authentic-sounding Italian operas, and so had tended to specialise in instrumental composition based on the inflexible academic models of the late Baroque era. However, they too gradually became adept at composing in the Italian style, as a result partly of the teaching of Italian émigrés, and partly of prolonged periods spent in Italy itself.

Mozart drew extensively on this international Italian style after becoming aware of its possibilities at an early age and in a number of different ways. Even at the age of five he had begun composing simple piano pieces and small-scale sonatas for piano and violin under his father's guidance, and when in London, aged only eight, he had already written his first symphonies by the end of 1764 or early in

On the left: "Le Nozze di Figaro", a scene from Act 1. Theatermuseum, Munich.

Below: poster advertising the premiere of the opera at the Vienna Hoftheater on 1 May 1786. Österreichische Nationalbibliothek, Vienna.

lody had to provide opportunities for virtuoso display on the part of the singer; that is, it had to serve as a vehicle for the technical and virtuoso embellishments that every successful singer was obliged to demonstrate. Thus, a melody had to satisfy the following requirements: it had to be singable, in the sense that it possessed a flowing, recognisable shape; it had to be expressive, able to convey an emotional situation or mood virtually instantaneously; and finally, it had to provide a basis for virtuoso variation and display without in any way losing its original identity and shape. In a sense, then, song had to be a perfect expressive medium, a language that could be understood wherever it was heard.

Opera buffa, on the other hand, had reduced virtuoso display in favour of greater realism, and so made use of a less imposing type of stylised conversation appropriate to rapid exchanges of 'speech'. One outcome of this process was the invention of a new melodic genre, the allegro cantabile.

These stylistic elements derived partly from the great Italian violin tradition of the late seventeenth century and early eighteenth centu-

1765. His early symphonies were more advanced than his father's, almost certainly because he had just met Johann Christian Bach, J.S. Bach's youngest son, who had quickly arrived at the concept of the modern symphony during a lengthy visit to Italy (where he had been admired as a composer of Italian operas). The ease and rapidity with which the young Mozart intuitively grasped and assimilated the principles of what was still a fledgeling musical form shows quite extraordinary musical insight and maturity. Dissatisfied with the popular German symphonic format of four 'academic' movements featuring fugal writing, rapid scales and arpeggios in fast movements, and uniform thematic treatment throughout, he preferred the three-movement format (allegro, andante, presto) of Italian opera overtures with three extremely short movements gravitating around an opening allegro dominated by the lively cantabile material of opera buffa. His employment of opera buffa material in these earliest symphonies is as much a matter of expressive and psychological need as of purely formal or stylistic preference. He conceived the symphony as not just another competently written piece of music, but as a

On the right: Simon Quaglio's stage design for the German premiere in Mannheim on 27 September 1789. Theatermuseum, Munich.

Below: printed ticket for the premiere of "Don Giovanni" in Prague on 29 October 1789. Theatermuseum, Munich.

living organism, a sequence of closely inter-related musical episodes. The three movements of his early symphonies soon became four when he added a minuet before the closing presto, but he never entirely abandoned the three-movement symphony. No less than 18 of his symphonies, including the monumental **Prague** Symphony, K. 504, of 1786, have only three movements.

After the symphony, his preferred orchestral genre was the concerto for solo instrument and orchestra, although his symphonic writing always remained more advanced and innovative. The standard concerto form of his day was modelled on the compositions of Vivaldi and other Baroque composers, in which contrasting blocks of material are discussed by the orchestra and a soloist or group of soloists. Mozart, too, at first adopted this model in his early piano concertos (for example, K. 107) which again show the influence of Johann Christian Bach. However, his first thoroughly personal piano concerto (K. 175) dates from December 1773 and shows the extent to

which he had left behind the concerto format he had been using only a few years earlier. There is a new relationship between piano and orchestra, a continuous dialogue rather than a simple opposition or contrast of forces, and thematic material is subtly inter-related. In the finale, the material is even reworked in contrapuntal fashion, an essentially collaborative rather than contrastive mode in which all thematic elements and lines have equal musical importance.

Mozart's astonishing powers of assimilation and synthesis are also evident in his German operas. When he came to use it, the **Singspiel** had been in existence for only a few years. The first German adaptation of the French opéra-comique (essentially a play with incorporated musical elements) dates from 1750. Mozart's earliest attempt at **Singspiel** is Bastien und Bastienne (1768), a simple and rather brittle small-scale opera. At the same time, however, other German composers were attempting to inject stronger dramatic content into German opera: Wieland's L'Alceste (1773) was set to music by

A scene from "Così fan tutte" in the 1983 La Scala production.
Ente Autonomo Teatro alla Scala, Milan.

Poster advertising the premiere of Mozart's opera buffa "Così fan tutte" in Vienna in 1791.
Österreichische Nationalbibliothek, Vienna.

Simon Quaglio's stage-design for Mozart's
"The Abduction from the Seraglio".
Theatermuseum, Munich.
J. Schaffer's stage-design for Mozart's "The Magic Flute".
Theatermuseum, Salzburg.

Schweitzer, Klein's Günther von Schwartzburg (1777) by Holz-bauer, and Wieland's Rosmunda (1778) by Schweitzer. Mozart was particularly impressed by the expressive and dramatic content of the last two of these operas, which seemed to herald the creation of a truly autonomous German opera tradition to rival Italian opera seria. Mozart wrote two **Singspiel** between 1779 and 1780: incidental music for Gebler's heroic play Thamos King of Egypt, and an unfinished light comic opera, Zaïde, of Turkish inspiration which served as a testing ground for the later Die Entführung aus dem Serail (1782), in which **Singspiel** first became an art form in its own right.

Had he been commissioned to do so, Mozart would undoubtedly have composed many other German operas, but in fact he wrote only one more, The magic flute in 1791, the last year of his life. The term **Singspiel** is no longer adequate to describe Mozart's great operas, which retain only the basic alternation of song and speech of the older theatrical form. We can now confidently speak of 'grand opera', the emergence of a new theatrical form incorporating elements of opera seria, opera buffa, the **Singspiel** of popular theatre, and the earlier German opera invented by Wieland but actually produced by Mozart in **Thamos**. The German opera tradition established by Mozart would later be developed by Weber, and culminate in the monumental works of Richard Wagner.

Vocal		

Sacred

1 oratorio	La Betulia liberata	1771
2 cantatas	Grabmusik	1767
	Davide penitente	1785
18 masses (2 fragmentary)	including:	
	Mass in C minor	1769
	Mass in C major (Dominicus-Messe)	1769
	Mass in C major (Credo-Messe)	1776
	Mass in C major (Krönungs-Messe)	1779
	Missa solemnis in C major	1780
	Mass in C minor (fragment)	1782-83
1 requiem	Requiem in D minor	1791
11 kyrie (6 unfinished)	including:	
	Kyrie in D major	1774
	Kyrie in D minor	1781
approx. 40 other works (some unfinished and/ or doubtful)	including:	
	7 offertories	1766-77
	4 lithanies	1771-76
	2 vespers	1779-80
	Regina Coeli	1791

Secular

3 cantatas	Dir, Sele de Weltalls (fragment)	1785
	Die Maurenfreude	1785
	Eine kleine Freymauer-Kantate	1791
other works for voice & orch.	including:	
	37 soprano arias	1765-89
	4 duets	1767-90
	10 terzettos	1783-88
	2 quartets	1785-89
approx. 50 canons (some very doubtful)	including:	
	Five enigmatic canons	1770
	Eight canons	

Songs		

approx. 40 songs	including:	
	Die grossmütige Gelassenheit	1772
	An die Eisamkeit	1780
	An die Hoffnung	1780
	Gesellenreise	1785
	Das Veilchen	1785
	Lied der Freiheit	1786
	Die Alte	1787
	Die Verschweigung	1787
	Das Lied der Trennung	1787
	Das Traumbild	1787
	Beim Auszug in das Feld	1788
	Das Kinderspiel	1791
	Eine kleine deutsche Kantate	1791

Piano		

22 sonatas	including:	
	B flat major K. 281	1774
	G major K. 283	1774
	D major K. 284 (Dürnitz-Sonate)	1775
	A minor K. 310	1778
	C major K. 330	1778
	A major K. 331	1778
	F major K. 332	1778
	C minor K. 457	1784
	C major K. 545	1788
	B flat major K. 570	1789
	C major K. 576	1789
17 sets of variations	including:	
	Twelve variations on 'Ah, vous dirai-je, Maman'	1778
	Eight variations on 'Ein Weib ist das herrlichste Ding'	1791
6 sonatas for piano duet	C major K. 19d	1765
	D major K. 381	1772
	B flat major K. 358	1774
	F major K. 497	1786
	G major K. 357	1786
	C major K. 521	1787
1 sonata for two pianos	D major K. 448	1781

Beethoven

Portrait of Beethoven by Joseph Karl Stieler, 1820. Beethovenhaus, Bonn.

When Ludwig van Beethoven was born in 1770 in Bonn, the pretty town on the banks of the Rhine, it had an important music Kappel, or chapel, in which the Beethovens, a family of musicians, were employed. They were of Flemish origin, which explains the *van* of Beethoven's surname. His grandfather, also called Ludwig, held the important post of Hofkappelmeister in the court orchestra, but his father was an undistinguished choral singer. Perhaps because he had been less than suc-cessful in his own career, his father did everything to give his son a sound musical education. He was merciless in his supervision of his piano playing, and made him perform in public as a child prodigy on 26 March 1778, when he was only seven. Later, the young Ludwig was handed over to Christian Gottlob Neefe, a qualified music teacher who was also court organist. Seeing that the boy had immense talent, Neefe taught him organ and composition as well as the piano. Beethoven was a

Portrait of the young Beethoven during his Bonn years. Beethovenhaus, Bonn.

willing and enthusiastic pupil, and soon attracted notice at the court, deputising occasionally for his teacher at the organ, playing harpsichord in the orchestra and singing with his father in the choir. In 1784, Beethoven was appointed deputy organist, a post that gave him a regular salary, but in the meantime his father had been dismissed after losing his voice completely (we know this from the Kappel records). This probably accounts for his subsequent moral and physical decline which led to the alcoholism and heavy debts his son seems rather to have despised him for.

Beethoven's early life was not enlivened by extensive travel, as Mozart's was. Apart from a brief stay in Vienna in 1787, where it is said he may have met and been praised by Mozart (although there is no documentation whatever to support this claim), it can probably be said that he spent the first 25 years of his life in his native Bonn. In any event, his stay in Vienna was curtailed by the death of his mother, which obliged him to return home.

Two years later, in 1789, Beethoven enrolled as a philosophy student at Bonn University and attended classes for a while. His acquaintance with the university intellectuals there helped to produce in him the remarkable self-knowledge and self-es-

teem that would make him one of the first consciously 'liberated' artists of modern times. Once settled in Vienna, Beethoven transformed the artist's role from that of the servant of a rich patron into that of a free agent, willing to compose only when he wished, who regarded the aristocracy of his day with the haughty dignity that comes of knowing his own worth.

By the time the young Beethoven was preparing to move to Vienna towards the end of 1792, some of his compositions were already circulating in Bonn. They were few in number, but clearly of some merit if we remember that Haydn himself had had encouraging words to say to the young composer after hearing his *Cantata for the death of the Emperor Joseph II* (no. 87) in 1790 during his brief stay in Bonn. However, the most interesting composition of this early period is the Octet in E flat, Op. 103, for oboes, clarinets, horns and bassoons. The *Balletto cavalleresco* of 1790 was first performed on 6 March 1791 in the reception rooms in Bonn.

Beethoven made influential friends during his final years in Bonn. The closest, Franz Gerhard Wegeler, introduced him to the aristocratic Breuning family as a piano teacher for their young children; another, Count Ferdinand Ernst von Waldstein, was the dedicatee of the *Waldstein* Sonata, Op. 53 (also known as the ***Aurora***, particularly in France).

The 22-year-old musician who left Bonn (he would never return) for Vienna, the musical as well as

The Breuning family home. Watercolour by M. Friekel. Stadarchiv, Bonn.

A set of silhouettes of the Breuning family. Beethovenhaus, Bonn.

political capital of the Empire, was already both an outstanding virtuoso pianist and a remarkable keyboard improviser, but he was soon to become the musical idol of Vienna.

Restless by nature, Beethoven was given to rudeness and could appear boorish because he had difficulty in expressing himself in words. This was certainly the immediate impression of Haydn, who did not approve of the undisciplined romanticism of some of his music, and may even have pointed out technical weaknesses in the compositions he saw during their lessons together. Arrogant and intolerant, Beethoven typically recalled: 'Yes, he [Haydn] gave me some lessons, but he taught me nothing'. His studies with Johann Georg Albrechtsberger, his counterpoint teacher, and the Italian opera writer Antonio Salieri were a good

The Prater in Vienna. Early 19th-century print. Albertina Graphische Sammlungen, Vienna.

deal more profitable, however.

We could almost say that Beethoven's period of apprenticeship came to an end in 1795 when, already well known as a pianist, he decided to establish himself officially in Vienna as a composer. His three Piano Trios, Op. 1, probably performed privately early in 1794 at the home of Prince Lichnovsky, a prominent Viennese nobleman, were published by Artaria in the same year. Beethoven had been staying with Lichnovsky since the early months of his residence in Vienna, and continued to receive an annual stipend of 600 florins from him (perhaps until as late as 1806), an act of disinterested patronage on Lichnovsky's part, with no specific duties expected in return. As well as the Trios, Beethoven also dedicated the Piano Sonata in C minor (*Pathétique*) of 1798-99, his *Variations on a theme of Paisello* and the Second Symphony of 1800-03 to his generous patron.

Other important early works include the three Piano Sonatas, Op. 2, dedicated to Haydn. The minuet of the First Sonata in F minor, the largo of the Second in A major, and the scherzo of the Third in C major, are particularly fine.

Beethoven performed his Second Piano Concerto in B flat, Op. 19, at the Burgtheater on 29 March 1795 and the following day gave a series of brilliant improvisations. The success he enjoyed then proved lasting, and also persuaded him to try his luck further afield in Prague and Berlin. This period marks the height of Beethoven's fame as a pianist, for he was earning considerable prestige in the musical world as well as substantial sums of money. He was no longer the poor musician who, on arriving in Vienna in 1792, had been hard put to find even the price of a dinner, comforted only by the private knowledge that he was a great pianist and composer, even if others were rather slow in seeing it. Now he was virtually run off his feet with work, but did his utmost to satisfy the endless requests for performances, although he had occasional bouts of bad temper.

In Berlin he was presented to Wilhelm Friedrich II, a keen music-lover and competent cellist. Pleased with the interview, Beethoven wrote the Cello Sonatas, Op. 5 (1796) in F major and G minor, urbane works demonstrating his mature command of chamber music writing. Other important compositions were written during this period, including the scene and aria *Ah! Perfido*, Op. 65, for soprano (1796), *Adelaide*, Op. 46, a cantata for piano and chorus (1797), and the Sonata in E flat major, Op. 7 (1797). The First Piano Concerto in C major, Op. 15 (1798), is a virtuoso piece with brilliant orchestral writing and impressively seductive piano phrasing.

At the start of the new century, Beethoven was fulfilled as a composer and self-assured as a man. In a letter to his friend Franz Wegeler in Bonn dated 29 June 1801, he wrote: 'My compositions are earning a lot and I've got more commissions than I can handle. Six or seven publishers are after every piece I've written, and there could be more if I wished ...'. However, the enthusiasm of the letter is dampened somewhat by a passing reference to his health which, with hindsight, strikes a chilling note: '... my hearing has got weaker of late ... my ears buzz and hum night and day ...'. None

The Artaria family. Österreichische Nationalbibliothek, Vienna.

of this is evident in the works he wrote in this period, especially the Septet in E flat major, Op. 20, for clarinet, bassoon, horn, violin, viola, cello and double bass, one of his most popular works on account of its simplicity and gentle wit. Essentially a serenade, Beethoven later transcribed it for clarinet, cello and piano (Op. 38).

The same easy-going style, although now on a larger scale, is found in the First Symphony in C major, Op. 21, first performed on 2 April 1800 at the National Theatre in Vienna. The Second Symphony in D major, Op. 36, was begun in the same year and finished in 1802. Other works of this period include the Variations for piano, two charming Romances for violin and orchestra (Op. 40 in G major and Op. 50 in F major), and the overture

The Kohlmarkt in Vienna, home of the Artaria publishing house, in a late 18th-century painting. Museum der Stadt, Vienna.

Title-page of "Three Trios for the Pianoforte" dedicated to the Prince Lichnovsky.
Bildarchiv der Österreichische Nationalbibliothek, Vienna.

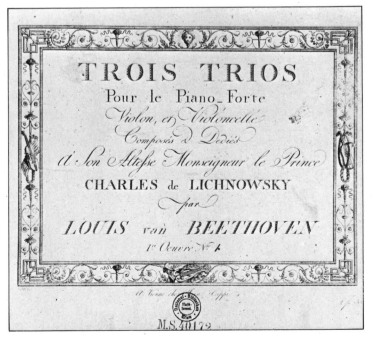

Above: Lobkovitzplatz in Vienna in a painting by Bernard Bellotto. Kunsthistorisches Museum, Vienna.

Below: the Prince and Princess Lobkovitz. Painting. Kunsthistorisches Museum, Vienna.

for the ballet *The creatures of Prometheus*, Op. 43, which seems to have been performed in a revised version at La Scala, Milan on 22 March 1813, the first time Beethoven's music had ever been played there.

In spite of occasional financial problems and fits of depression brought on by the tendency to isolate himself from his friends as his deafness worsened, these intensely creative years produced an untroubled flow of great music, including the Violin Sonatas in A minor, Op. 23, and F major ('The spring'), Op. 24, as well as the monumental Third Piano Concerto in C minor, Op. 37, and the six String Quartets, Op. 18, dedicated to Prince Lobkovitz. Similar in some ways to these quartets is the String Quintet in C major, Op. 29, composed early in 1800, a remarkable essay in string colouring and balance.

After completing his revision of the Op. 18 Quartets early in 1800, several years passed before Beethoven tried his hand again at quartet writing. The three Op. 59 String Quartets came in 1805, and the single Op. 74 Quartet in 1809. The Op. 95 Quartet, another isolated work, appeared in 1810, to be followed by the wonderful *Late Quartets*, perhaps his profoundest spiritual utterances, towards the end of his life.

Beethoven's creative development is well illustrated by the progression of his piano sonatas, but to understand them we must also appreciate Beethoven's unique position in the musical world of his time. It is usually said that Beethoven was an 'instrumentalist' by nature, and his writing for that medium is indeed formidable, at times carrying conventional sonata form to its utmost limits or even further.

Sonata form was the outcome of a lengthy formal and stylistic evolution to which composers over the years had contributed their various ways of handling themes and developing musical arguments, and the sonata form that flourished in the years from 1740 to 1760 had also undergone its own internal evolution. In this period, the term 'sonata form' was used to describe a piece of music for a solo instrument or two 'equal' instruments, one of which was usually the piano, but by the turn of the century the piano had become *the* sonata instrument. The range of expressive resources and the subtlety of tonal shading it offered (especially to master pianists such as Beethoven) made it ideal for a form in which harmonic experimentation and expressive and thematic contrast

were harnessed to psychological exploration and spiritual reflection, and Beethoven carried these aspects of it to new levels of technical sophistication and expressive subtlety.

When he turned to sonata form during his early years in Bonn, the result was the three Op. 2 Sonatas dedicated to Haydn, which gave immediate proof of Beethoven's command of the form. With the publication of the Sonata in C minor, Op. 2, in the autumn of 1799 under the title of *Grande sonate pathétique*, it became apparent that Beethoven's earlier skill had now developed into genius. Conversely, the two Op. 14 Sonatas published in 1799, and the Sonata in B flat major, Op. 22, published in 1802, seem to hark back to conventional eighteenth-century sonatas. The Sonata in A flat major, Op. 26 published in March 1802 once more abandons traditional forms, and the two *Sonate quasi una fantasia*, Op. 27 are even freer in conception. The C sharp minor sonata is usually known as the *Moonlight Sonata*, and the other in B flat major is dedicated to the Princess of Lichtenstein. Both are extremely free in form and explore new piano sonorities and timbres for the first time. The *Moonlight Sonata* has the hypnotic charm of a work that seems more the result of improvisation than formal composition, as if Beethoven were reflecting on his feelings for the young Giulietta Guicciardi.

Title-page of the first edition of the Beethoven concerto dedicated to Prince Lobkovitz. Österreichische Nationalbibliothek, Vienna.

Above: the crowning of Napoleon Bonaparte in Notre-Dame, Paris. Painting by Jacques Louis David. Louvre, Paris.
Below: title-page of the 3rd Symphony, "Eroica". Österreichische Nationalbibliothek, Vienna.

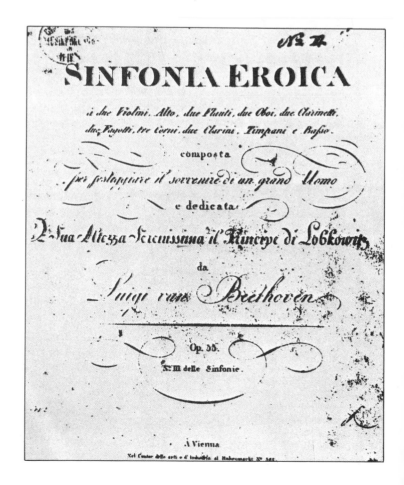

Other important sonatas of this period are the Sonata in C major (*Walstein* or *Aurora*), Op. 53, dedicated to his Bonn patron Count Waldstein, and the famous Sonata in A minor (*Appassionata*) which Beethoven regarded as his best sonata, perhaps because it reminded him of his unhappy love for Theresa Brunswick. The *Grande concerto concertante*, Op. 56, or *Triple Concerto* as it is usually known, for violin, piano and cello, marks a return to a more urbane, less uncompromising style of composition.

The Sonata in E flat major (*Les adieux*), Op. 81 of 1809 was followed in 1817 by the Sonata in E flat major (*Hammerklavier*), and then, in his final years, by the three great *Late Sonatas*, Opp. 109, 110 and 111, whose deceptive simplicity and melodic beauty seem to deny Beethoven's agonised rejection of his own physical deterioration in old age. The Op. 111 Sonata in C minor, composed in 1822 and dedicated to the Archduke Rudolph, is the last of Beethoven's 32 piano sonatas.

In addition to the piano sonatas, there are the ten Violin Sonatas and the five Cello Sonatas. The most famous of the violin sonatas is the *Kreutzer*, Op. 47, in which Beethoven makes great demands on the technical skill of the performer. The Cello Sonata in A major, Op. 69, dedicated to his friend Ignaz von Gleichenstein, is famous for its exquisite melodic lines.

Beethoven was busy with another important work round 1804, this time an opera. The birth of *Fidelio*, his only opera, was a long and agonising process. The premiere at the Theater an der Wien was a disaster, but after condensing and revising some of its material for the third of the overtures he wrote for it (*Eleonora Overture No. 3*), he took up the opera again in 1806. It was performed in a radically revised version in 1814. Much to Beethoven's satisfaction, the opera became justly popular during his later life.

As well as starting work on his only opera, Beethoven had also begun to compose the Fourth Symphony, Op. 60, in 1806. Its strange mixture of serene confidence and an altogether darker kind of reticence is very different from the high drama of the earlier Third Symphony, written in 1803, to which Beethoven himself added the name *Eroica*. Famous for its remarkable slow movement, a funeral march, the **Eroica** was inspired by the achievements of Napoleon Bonaparte as consul. When, however, Napoleon allowed himself to made Emperor in 1804, Beethoven crossed out his earlier dedication and wrote instead: '... composed in memory of a great man'.

As soon as the Fourth was finished, he immediately began work on the titanic Fifth Symphony in C minor, Op. 67, in the summer of 1807. Returning to it in 1808, he completed it at the same time as the Sixth Symphony. The massive Fifth is famous for the powerful rhythm of its opening theme. The Sixth Symphony (*Pastoral*) in F major, Op. 68,

Simon Quaglio, stage-design for a performance of Beethoven's "Fidelio" in 1820. Theatermuseum, Munich.

'more an expression of what the senses feel than a picture of nature' as Beethoven's autograph notes make clear, is, with the *Pathétique* and *Les adieux* piano sonatas, one of the very few works to which Beethoven himself attached a name.

His only Violin Concerto in D major, Op. 61, was written immediately after the Fifth Symphony, and the splendid Fourth Piano Concerto in G major, Op. 58, came in 1806. The *Coriolanus Overture* of 1807, written for the tragedy of the same name by the German poet Collin, is notable for its conceptual grandeur and dramatic power. His other famous overture, *Egmont*, Op. 84, was written in 1810. Full of violent tension and drama, it is a measure of Beethoven's admiration for Goethe, to whom he wrote on 12 April 1811: '... *Egmont*, which I felt and reflected upon and then set to music with the same enthusiasm as I had read it ...'.

Beethoven's output in 1809, the year in which the Napoleonic War shattered the calm of Viennese life, was obviously not very large, but he did write the Fifth Piano Concerto in E flat major, Op. 73,

Above: portrait of Beethoven by Joseph Mahler painted around 1804-1805. Beethovenhaus, Bonn.
Below left: portrait of Giulietta Guicciardi by an unknown artist. Miniature. Beethovenhaus, Bonn.
Below right: title-page of Beethoven's "Sonata quasi una fantasia" for pianoforte, Op. 27 no. 2, usually known as the "Moonlight" sonata. Beethoven Archiv, Bonn.

dedicated to the Archduke Rudolph in gratitude for his patronage. Known as the *Emperor*, this virtuoso concerto moves from the massive solemnity of the opening allegro through the hushed intensity of its adagio to the uninhibited triumph of its Rondo finale.

A philosophical cast of mind and an extraordinary revival of his creative powers helped Beethoven to overcome the fits of black depression that occasionally overwhelmed him as his hearing gradually deteriorated. The outcome of this in the period from 1810 to 1811 was the wonderful Piano Trio in B flat major, Op. 97, dedicated to the Archduke Rudolph, and the stupendous Seventh Symphony in A major, Op. 92, famous for its pulsating rhythms, especially in the extraordinary finale. Between late 1811 and the summer of 1812 he was also able to finish the Eighth Symphony in F major, Op. 93, a small-scale work that combines eighteenth-century grace with highly original musical argument.

After the temporary triumph of his bombastic *Victory of Wellington* of 1813, which even includes cannon shots, Beethoven entered an especially dark period in his life. '... the many unhappy events that have befallen me,' he wrote, 'have reduced me virtually to a mental wreck.' On the death of his brother Kaspar he was awarded care of his young nephew Karl, who proved extremely fickle and difficult to handle. Moreover, his deafness was now almost total. 'Sometimes I can hear sounds,' he confessed to friends, 'but I can't hear words any more ...'. In order to converse, he began to ask his friends to write down their answers to his questions in his notebooks, which became the famous 'conversation books' found among his papers after his death.

In spite of his physical decline, he began work on the Ninth Symphony in the autumn of 1822. An illness-ridden 1823 produced, miraculously enough, two great masterpieces, the *Missa solemnis*, Op. 123, and the *Thirty-three variations on a waltz by Diabelli*, Op. 120, for piano, the one a towering assertion of faith, the other his definitive statement on the technical resources of the piano. The Ninth Symphony in D minor, Op. 125, was completed in 1824 and dedicated to Wilhelm Friedrich III of Prussia. It proved difficult to write.

Title-page of the piano transcription of "The Victory of Wellington" or "The Victory Battle", published by Steiner. Österreichische Nationalbibliothek, Vienna.

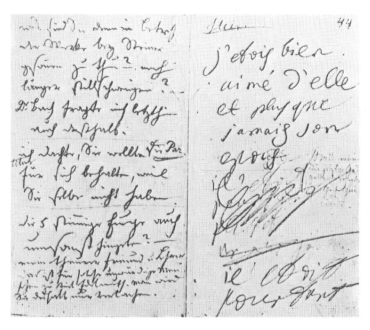

Autograph page of Beethoven's "Conversation Books".
Beethovenhaus, Bonn.

side world. The very last Quartet, Op. 135, dates from late 1826. Beethoven died on 26 March 1827. The funeral was impressive: more than twenty thousand people accompanied his bier, including a young mourner named Franz Schubert, who was to follow him to the grave a mere year later. Vienna was stunned when it suddenly realised that Ludwig van Beethoven, that shabby, irascible individual who had absent-mindedly roamed the streets of the city and always seemed to be changing address, was a great genius to whom they should have bowed their heads in homage.

The first sketches date from 1817, and he abandoned it but later took it up again in 1822. Twelve years separate the Eighth and Ninth Symphonies, which explains the many innovative features of his last symphony, (it has much freer harmonic and thematic development and also a looser structure than his earlier symphonies). In the last movement, for example, he introduces a choir and soloists who sing Schiller's *Ode to joy*. It was first performed in the Kèrntnertortheater in Vienna on 7 May 1824 in a memorable concert during which, as a witness said, Beethoven 'took part by conducting the orchestra'. He may have taken part, but he certainly did not conduct, because by that time he was stone deaf, unable even to hear the loud applause of the audience. For him, all was now silence.

It may well have been thought at the time that the Ninth Symphony would mark the end of his composing career. What could possibly come after this? Moreover, Beethoven was tired, in pain, and physically weak. And yet, just a short while afterwards, his physical and mental exhaustion did nothing to prevent him from writing the wonderful *Late Quartets*, justly regarded perhaps as the most intimate and personal works he ever wrote, his final statement. Nothing could be more dramatic than this last desperate rejection of the out-

Title-page of the first edition of Beethoven's String Quartet in B flat major. Biblioteca del Conservatorio G. Verdi, Milan.

Beethoven's funeral in a watercolour by Franz Stöber. Beethovenhaus, Bonn.

Stage

1 opera	Fidelio (3 versions)	1805, 1806, 1814
2 ballets	Musik du einem Ritterballet	1790-91
	The Creatures of Prometheus	1801
incidental music	including:	
	Egmont (Goethe), overture & nine pieces	1810
	The Ruins of Athens (von Kotzebue), overture & eight pieces	1811
	King Stephen (von Kotzebue), overture & nine pieces	1811
	The Consecration of the House (Meisl), overture & nine pieces (see also Overtures under Orchestral)	1811-12

Orchestral

9 symphonies	No. 1 in C major	1799-1800
	No. 2 in D major	1800-03
	No. 3 in E flat minor ('Eroica')	1803
	No. 4 in B flat major	1806
	No. 5 in C minor	1804-08
	No. 6 in F major ('Pastoral')	1807-08
	No. 7 in A major	1811-12
	No. 8 in F major	1812
	No. 9 in D minor	1822-24
3 overtures	Leonora (3 versions)	1805-06
	Coriolanus	1807
	Namensfeier (see also Incidental music under Stage)	1814
various works	including:	
	24 German dances	1795-1800c
	30 minuets	1795-99
	12 controddanzas	1800-01
	Wellington's Victory	1813

Instrumental

concertos (and romances)	5 piano concertos	
	- No. 1 in C major	1795-98
	- No. 2 in B flat major	1795-98
	- No. 3 in C minor	1800
	- No. 4 in G major	1805-06
	- No. 5 in E flat major ('Emperor')	1808-09
	Violin concerto in D major	1806
	Triple concerto in C major for violin, cello and piano	1804-05
	2 romances for violin & orch. (G major & F major)	1802
	Fantasia in C minor for piano, chorus & orch.	1808

Piano

32 sonatas	including:	
	Sonata in C minor ('Pathétique')	1798-99
	Sonata quasi una fantasia in C sharp minor ('Moonlight')	1801
	Sonata in D major ('Pastoral')	1801
	Sonata in C major ('Waldstein')	1803-04
	Sonata in F minor ('Appassionata')	1804-05
	Sonata in E flat major ('Les adieux')	1809
	Sonata in A major Op. 101	1816
	Sonata in E flat major ('Hammerklavier')	1817-19
	Sonata in E major Op. 109	1820
	Sonata in A flat major Op. 110	1821
	Sonata in C minor Op. 111	1821-22
21 sets of variations	including:	
	15 variations and fugue on a theme from 'Prometheus'	1802
	32 variations on an original theme	1806
	33 variations on a waltz by Diabelli	1819-23
approx. 50 misc. pieces	including:	
	11 bagatelles	1800-22
	7 bagatelles	1802c
	Fantasia in G minor	1809
	Bagatelle in A minor ('Für Elise')	1810
	Polonaise in C major	1814
	6 bagatelles	1823-24

Chamber

16 string quartets	Six quartets Op. 18	1798-1801
	Three quartets Op. 59	1805-06
	Quartet Op. 74	1809
	Quartet Op. 95	1810
	Quartet Op. 127	1825
	Quartet Op. 132	1825
	Quartet Op. 130 (with Grosse Fuge)	1825-26
	Quartet Op. 131	1826
	Quartet Op. 135	1826
other string works	including:	
	3 quintets	
	3 trios	
10 violin sonatas	Three sonatas (D, A, E flat)	1797-98
	Sonata in A minor	1800-01
	Sonata in F major ('The Spring')	1800-01
	Three sonatas (A, C minor, G)	1802
	Sonata in A major ('Kreutzer')	1802-03
	Sonata in G major	1812-13
5 cello sonatas	Two sonatas (F major, G minor)	1796
	Sonata in A major	1807-08
	Two sonatas (C major, D major)	1815
13 piano trios	including:	
	Trio in G major (piano, flute, bassoon)	1786-90
	Trio in E flat major (piano, violin, cello)	1790-91c
	Three trios (piano, violin, cello)	1793-94
	Trio in B flat major (piano, clar., cello)	1798
	Trio in E flat major (piano, clar., cello)	1802-03
	Two trios (piano, violin, cello)	1800
	Trio in B flat major (piano, violin, cello) ('Archduke')	1811
works for piano & wind	Quintet for piano, oboe, clarinet, bassoon and horn	1796-97
	Horn sonata	1800
works for wind	Octet in E flat major	1792
	Sextet in E flat major	1796
	Rondino in E flat major	1796
	Trio in C major	1794
	Three duets for clarinet and bassoon	1790-92c
other mixed chamber works	Septet in E flat major	1799-1800
	Sextet in E flat major	1794-95
	Three quartets for piano, violin, viola & cello	1785

Vocal

2 masses	Mass in C major	1807
	Missa Solemnis	1819-23
1 oratorio	Christ on the Mount of Olives	1803-04
8 cantatas	including:	
	Cantata on the death of Joseph II	1790
	Der glorreiche Augenblick	1814
	Calm Sea and Prosperous Voyage	1814-15
3 scenes & arias for soprano & orchestra	Ah, perfido!	1795-96
	Primo amore	1800c
	No, non turbarti	1801-02
30 chamber works	including:	
	26 Italian songs	1792-1802
approx. 90 songs for voice & piano	including:	
	Eight songs (Claudius, Goethe, Bürger, Lessing & others)	1790-93
	Six songs (Gellert)	1803
	In questa tomba oscura	1807
	Six songs (Goethe)	1809
	Three songs (Goethe)	1810
	An die ferne Geliebte (cycle by Jeitteles)	1816
	Ruf vom Berge (Treitschke)	1816
approx. 50 canons		1795-1826

Schubert

Portrait of Franz Schubert. Gesellschaft der Musikfreunde, Vienna.

Franz Schubert was born in Vienna on 31 January 1797 into a family of Bohemian origin. Although he spent most of his brief life in the Hapsburg capital, he never became a leading figure in the musical life of the city, and during his lifetime never enjoyed the kind of popularity granted to other composers no less great than he – Haydn, Beethoven and Brahms, to name only a few.

Born with an extraordinary aptitude for music, Franz received his first musical tuition from his father, a primary school teacher and competent violinist and cellist, and then from his brother Ignaz. In 1804, at the age of seven, he was sent to the organist of the church of Lichtenthal in Vienna. When they realised just how gifted he was, his family looked for ways to provide him with a more thorough musical education, given that he already played the violin extremely well. The timely granting of an educational scholarship enabled the less than well-off Schubert family to send Franz to the

Schubert's birthplace in the Lichtenthal district of Vienna, in a print by Michael Eder. Gesellschaft der Musikfreunde, Vienna.

Vienna Stadtkonvikt (Imperial and Royal City College) whose teaching staff included, among other important tutors, the famous opera composer and court musician, Antonio Salieri. Discipline was strict and the teaching severe, and Franz may well have suffered on account of his lack of money, but these early years were crucial to his musical development.

The Stadtkonvikt had a small student orchestra which met daily. Schubert played in the second, and later in the first violin sections. His earliest compositions date from this period. We know of a Fantasia for piano duet dating almost certainly from 1810 when he was still only a child.

Both his skill at and love for composition are evident from other works written around 1812-13, *Lieder* and string quartets composed for musical

evenings at the Schubert home with his father playing the cello and three of his sons, Ignaz, Ferdinand and Franz, playing violins and the piano. Schubert left the Stadtkonvikt at the age of 16 and went to the training institute for elementary teachers in the Annegasse, where he took the teaching certificate that would enable him to teach, like his father, in elementary schools. Such work was unlikely to satisfy the ambitious young composer, but it was always a way of earning money: financial difficulties and a Bohemian way of life were to be constant features throughout the rest of his life. However, the dullness of his daily routine never made him lose sight of music, for which he felt himself naturally gifted. During the three years he spent teaching small children, Schubert produced a number of true masterpieces: two String Quar-

Schubert at the age of sixteen. Drawing.
Schubert Schule, Vienna.

tets, several symphonies, the Mass No. 1 in F major, some piano sonatas and six stage works. The Mass was sung in the parish church of Lichtenthal on 16 October 1814 by the young singer Therese Grob, with whom Franz fell in love.

In the meantime, his output was gradually improving in both quality and quantity. On 19 October 1814 he wrote his first really great song, *Gretchen am Spinnrade* (Gretchen at the wool-winder), based on Goethe's text. In the following year he wrote 145 **Lieder** and 4 **Singspiele**. He composed furiously, producing a stream of song and other works, but none was commissioned so he made no money whatever from them, in spite of the fact that his more than 600 songs on texts by Goethe, Heine, Schiller, Platen and other lesser poets of his time are now regarded as some of the most beautiful songs ever written (to say nothing of the wonderful instrumental music he also composed throughout his life).

Schubert's application for the post of music teacher at the Laibach school in Slovenia was unsuccessful, but further readings of Goethe in 1816 produced another crop of splendid songs, including *Erlkönig* (The elf king) and *Gesänge des Harfners* (Songs of the harpist), as well as two new symphonies, the *Tragic* in C minor, and the Fifth in B flat major. In June 1816 he began a cantata, *Prometheus*, a work which, at long last, had actually been commissioned from him. He received what he regarded as the enormous sum of 100 florins.

On a visit to Linz in 1815, Schubert met a young, well educated man called Franz von Schober who was to become one of his closest friends in later life and radically change the course of his life. The son of well-to-do parents, von Schober led a brilliant social life, but was sensitive and open-minded enough to realise how much Schubert's morale and composing were being affected by his monotonous, badly paid job. Schubert was encouraged by von Schober to leave the school and come to live in his own home. Franz accepted, and in 1817 found himself a free composer in Vienna: from then on he would have to make his living from his musical activity, having broken with the constricting lower middle class world he had been used to until then. In Schober's home Schubert met the baritone Johann Michael Vogl, then at the height of his career, and together they organised musical evenings, the so-called **Schubertiaden**, which attracted smart Viennese society for some time. However, success

Franz von Schober, one of Schubert's closest friends, in an oil portrait by Leopold Kupelwieser. Schuber Museum, Vienna.

Schubert and his friends indulging in party games. Painting by Kupelwieser, 1821. Schubert Museum, Vienna.

and renown were slow in coming, and the 20-year-old Schubert realised the difficulty of his position: his work paid badly, and he had no home of his own.

Not surprisingly, the young composer willingly grasped the opportunity offered him when another of his many loyal friends, Anselm Hüttenbrenner, introduced him to Count Paul Anton Esterházy, a member of one of Hungary's oldest noble families. The nobleman offered him the post of music tutor to his two daughters and invited him to his family seat at Zseliz in Hungary. The stay in Hungary, enjoyable at first, quickly became boring and then unbearable, and was short-lived. Lack of friends, nostalgia for his beloved Vienna and little opportunity for music-making all made Schubert decide to return to Vienna in November 1818, where he ended up sharing a house with his friend, the poet Mayrhofer.

The summer of 1819 was a happy and productive one for Schubert. He travelled to Upper Austria accompanied by the singer Vogl, with whom he gave a series of small, carefully organised concerts featuring many of his songs, and organised musical evenings in the home of Sylvester Paumgartner, a wealthy inhabitant of the region. One composition he wrote for these evenings, the Piano Quintet in A major, also known as the *Trout Quintet* because the theme of its finale is taken from one of his songs, *Die Forelle* (The trout), has subsequently become one of his best-known pieces. He also wrote a new Piano Sonata in A major, Op. 120, and completed his one-act **Singspiel** *Die Zwillingsbrüder* (The twin brothers) and the music for the melodrama *Die Zauberharfe* (The magic harp), both of which were mounted the following year in Vienna. One of his greatest masterpieces, the *Quartettsatz* in C minor, was written in 1820, although it was published posthumously in 1870. He was able to have a collection of his songs published in 1820, together with another collection of 36 dances, and he composed a new opera, *Alfonso und Estrella*, which was never performed in his lifetime.

By this stage Schubert was beginning to be known in Vienna. Although publishers continued to ignore him on the whole, his works were performed from manuscript in private homes and at musical evenings. The autumn of 1822 saw the composition of the *Unfinished Symphony* in B minor, a work of extraordinary melancholy and beauty which, for unknown reasons, he never managed to complete. The score was accidentally restored to the world more than 60 years after it had been written by Schubert's old friend Anselm Hüttenbrenner, who happened to find it in a drawer. The same year also saw the completion of the Mass in A flat major and the *Wanderer fantasy* for piano, so called because, again, it is based on the theme of another of Schubert's own songs, *Der Wanderer*.

1823 got off to a very promising start, with Schubert now convinced that he was a mature all-round composer as well as an accomplished writer of songs. His compositions of this year included incidental music for *Rosamunde, Fürstin von Cypern* (Rosamund, Princess of Cyprus) and the first of his three song-cycles, *Die schöne Müllerin*. 1824 began with three chamber masterpieces: the String Quartet in A minor, the String Quartet in D minor (*Death and the maiden*) and the *Octet*. He composed various works for piano duet during the summer, including the famous *Divertissement à la hongroise* (Hungarian divertimento), the Sonata in C major (Gran duo), Op. 140, the *Eight variations on an original*

Above: Schubert and Vogl, the famous singer and champion of his music, in an amusing caricature of the time. Schubert Museum, Vienna.

Below: Franz Schubert on an outing to the country with friends. Watercolour by Leopold Kupelwieser, 1820. Schubert Museum, Vienna.

theme, Op. 35, the *Four Ländler* and the *Six grandes marches en trio*. All these works were written in the year in which Schubert accepted Count Esterházy's new offer to become tutor to his two daughters, and although his financial situation was now a good deal less than precarious, his state of mind had changed considerably. 'My peace has vanished,' he wrote, 'I shall never, never find it again.' He was a changed man, and increasingly aware of a gradual loss of his physical powers as the syphilis he had contracted earlier in life began to take hold of him. The disease was incurable then and, aggravated by an attack of typhoid fever, was eventually to kill him.

As periods of unexpected improvement alternated with gradual decline, Schubert continued to write music, now his only consolation and reason for remaining alive. Between 1825 and the early months of 1826 he completed a number of important works, including the Piano Sonata in A minor, Op. 42, the Piano Sonata in D major, Op. 53, and his last Symphony in C major, *The Great*. Possibly composed as late as 1828, this symphony remained unknown until 1839, when Schumann found the manuscript among some of Schubert's papers. The period from 1827, the year of Beethoven's death, and the au-

tumn of 1828, when Schubert died, saw the composition of a whole series of perhaps Schubert's greatest masterpieces. Summoning what little remained of his physical strength, he had the honour of escorting Beethoven to his grave on 27 March 1827, and seems to have been given a new lease of creative life as a result. The exhausting months that followed produced his second song-cycle, *Winterreise* (Winter journey), based on poems by Müller, four Impromptus for piano, Op. 90, the Trio in B flat major, Op. 99, and the Fantasia for violin and piano, Op. 159.

The 14 songs of his third song-cycle, *Schwanengesang* (Swan-song) certainly date from 1828, together with his last three piano sonatas and the String Quintet (with two cellos) in C major.

The Viennese musical world failed on the whole to appreciate the quality of this final burst of extraordinary masterpieces. The works remained either unknown or, if known, were considered too long. Even worse, they were often savagely cut. In 1828, a reviewer for the *Allgemeine Musikalische* was able to write: '... a new Fantasia, Op. 159, aroused not the slightest interest ... the composer has lost his way'. Heavily in debt, ridiculed by the critics, and now seriously ill, Schubert attempted to organise a

Happy times at Atzenburg. Watercolour by Leopold Kupelwieser. Gesellschaft der Musikfreunde, Vienna.

Illustration by R. Schuster and A. Baurmann for an 1878 edition of "Die Schöne Müllerin".

concert of his own music entirely for his own benefit on 26 March 1828 to mark the anniversary of Beethoven's death. Fortunately, it was a success and the proceeds enabled him to pay off his debts and even buy a new piano. It was, perhaps, the last happy event of his life.

A sudden improvement in his health early in October gave him the idea of going to Eisenstadt to visit Haydn's grave there. He suffered a relapse on returning to Vienna, and wrote in desperation to Schober on 12 November: 'I am ill. I have eaten nothing for 11 days and drunk nothing, and I totter feebly and shakily from my chair to my bed and back again'. Schubert died on 19 November 1828 and was buried near the body of Beethoven in the Währing cemetery.

A silhouette of Schubert at the piano.
Österreichische Nationalbibliothek, Vienna.

Stage		
2 operas	Alfonso und Estrella	1821-22
	Fierabras	1823
7 Singspiele	including:	
	Claudina di Villa Bella	1815
	Fernando	1815
	Gli amici di Salamanca (Salamanca's Friends)	1815
	I gemelli (The Twins)	1819
incidental music and/or operettas	including:	
	Rosamunde	1823

Orchestral		
9 symphonies & fragments	including:	
	D major	1815
	C minor ('Tragic')	1816
	C major	1818
	B minor ('Unfinished')	1822
	C major ('The Great')	1828
11 overtures & fragments	including:	
	C major 'in the Italian style'	1817
	D major 'In the Italian style'	1817
	E minor	1819
various works	including:	
	5 German Dances	1813

Chamber		
15 string quartets & fragments	including:	
	C minor (Quartettsatz)	1820
	A Minor	1824
	D minor ('Death and the Maiden')	1824
other string works	Trio in B flat major	1817
	Quintet in C major	1828
6 violin sonatas	including:	
	Fantasia in C major	1827
works for piano & other instruments	including:	
	Piano Quintet in A major ('Trout')	1819
string & wind works	including:	
	1 Wind Octet (Eine kleine Trauermusik)	1813

Piano		
19 sonatas (some unfinished)	including:	
	A minor	1823
	C major	1825
	D major	1825
	G major (Fantasia)	1826
	C minor	1828
	A major	1828
	B flat major	1828
approx. 500 misc. pieces (some lost, or fragments)	including:	
	approx. 100 Ländler	1815-24
	approx. 50 Waltzes	1815-28
	Wanderer Fantasia in C major	1822
	6 Moments Musicaux	1823-28c
	11 Impromptus	1827-28
various works for piano duet	including:	
	Divertissement à la hongroise	1824
	Sonata in C major (Grand Duo)	1824
	Rondo in A major	1828
	Fantasia in F minor	1828

Vocal		
8 masses	including:	
	Deutsche Trauermesse	1818
	Deutsche Messe	1826-27
approx. 40 other sacred works	including:	
	2 Stabat Mater	1815-16
	6 Antiphonies	1820
	7 Salve Regina	1812-24
	Hymn to the Holy Spirit	1828
80 choral works	including:	
	approx. 30 works for chamber choir	1812-28
approx. 60 works for 2 or 3 voices		

Songs		
approx. 600 songs	including:	
	Margerita all'arcolaio	1814
	Erlkönig	1816
	Die schöne Müllerin (20 songs)	1823
	Songs from Goethe's 'Wilhelm Meister' (4 songs)	1826
	Winterreise	1827
	Schwanengesang (13 songs)	1828

Berlioz

Portrait of Hector Berlioz by Gustave Courbet. Bibliothèque de l'Opéra, Paris.

Hector Berlioz was born at La Côte Saint André (Isère) on 9 December 1803 into a prosperous middle-class family. His father, a doctor, wanted him to study medicine, but he had little inclination for school work.

After completing his high-school studies in Grenoble, Berlioz moved to Paris at the age of 18, ostensibly to enrol at the University, but medicine did not prove much to his taste, although going to performances of Gluck and Spontini operas and studying scores in the library of the Paris Conservatory certainly did. By 1822 he had decided to abandon medicine and become a music critic, and study music with Jean-François Lesueur. He was an enthusiastic student, although he always regarded himself as a self-taught musician.

Berlioz' earliest compositions date from 1825. A Mass which he had performed at his own expense in the Church of St Rocco was moderately popular with the critics. It was followed by an opera, *Lénor ou Les Francs Juges*, of which we now have only the overture, and another piece which found its way into the later *Symphonie fantastique*.

He entered for the Prix de Rome for the first time in 1826, but never reached the final. Returning to Paris, he was accepted at the Conservatory where he studied composition with Lesueur and fugue with Reicha. He entered again for the Prix de Rome in 1827, and this time reached the final with his cantata *La mort d'Orphée* (The death of Orpheus). Impulsive by nature, he suddenly fell in love with English literature around 1827 as a result of seeing Shakespeare plays at the Odéon theatre in Paris. The performance of *Hamlet* was the social event of the season, and made Shakespeare Berlioz' favourite poet, although his enthusiasm was also partly the result of his infatuation with Harriet Smithson, the leading actress, whom he married in 1833.

Finally, in 1830, he won the Prix de Rome at his fifth attempt, and this brought him financial rewards, the chance to spend two years studying in Rome (with the obligation to produce at least two compositions), some important new friendships and, above all, official recognition that he was now a mature composer.

He was already fairly well known in France by then, in any case, because the premiere of the *Symphonie fantastique* at the Paris Conservatory on 5 December 1830 had been quite well received. The *Symphonie* was written in 1829 after Harriet Smithson had yet again refused the love which dominated him for the rest of his life. Not surprisingly, it is highly biographical, very much the kind of literature-inspired 'programme' piece that Berlioz had learned about from his first teacher. He himself published the 'programme' to coincide with the premiere, so the piece may be taken as an intentionally detailed description of the torment he was suffering at the time.

In addition to this first taste of Shakespearian theatre, another literary match that ignited the dry tinder of his fiery imagination was his reading of Goethe's *Faust* in the French translation by Gérard de Nerval. He spent 1828 and 1829 setting parts of it to music, and the result was *Huit scénes de Faust* (Eight scenes from Faust) for soloists, chorus and orchestra. The success of the premiere at the Paris Conservatory may have helped him to win the Prix

de Rome the following year.

Obliged to live in Rome on the grant he had been awarded in 1830 as winner of the Prix, Berlioz soon found that Italian life did not particularly agree with him. Indeed, he detested it so much that he longed to return to Paris where he had conceived another unfortunate passion, this time for the pianist Marie Moke. His hopes were dashed when she

Above: Berlioz' wife, the English actress Harriet Smithson, as Ophelia in Shakespeare's "Hamlet". 19th-century print by A. De Valmont. Bibliothèque de l'Opéra, Paris.

Below: Harriet Smithson as Juliet in Shakespeare's "Romeo and Juliet". Print, 1827.
Bibliothèque de l'Opéra, Paris.

Berlioz terrifies his audience with his "rowdy" music. Satirical engraving by A. Geiger. Österreichische Nationalbibliothek, Vienna.

left him to marry Camille Pleyel, the wealthy piano manufacturer, so he started composing furiously again, as he usually did in such cases. Having renounced all feelings of vindictiveness, he completed *Lélio ou Le rétour à la vie* (Lélio, or The return to life) in 1831. In many ways it was a sequel to the *Symphonie fantastique*, and the two pieces were in fact performed in the same concert in Paris the following year.

Having reconciled himself somewhat to life in Italy, Berlioz began to look around a little and soon discovered the art of Ancient Rome and the Renaissance, especially the architecture and sculpture, but he never managed to like Italian opera. We know that he remained indifferent to the art form that so many other musicians of his time found easy to love and admire.

He saw Harriet again on returning to Paris, and although she was no longer the beautiful and famous young actress he had fallen desperately in love with years before, he decided to marry her. The following year, financial difficulties forced him to step up his activity as a music critic, which

he did with some success because he was also a fluent and interesting writer. He wrote for the *Journal des débats*, where he remained until 1864, although he never lost sight of his musical vocation, and continued to compose.

1834 saw the completion of *Harold in Italy*, whose viola obligato part was specially written for Paganini, although he never actually performed it. Three years later, in 1837, came the *Grande Messe des morts*, usually known as the *Requiem*, which calls for unusually large orchestral and choral forces. His memories of his life in Rome emerged in an opera, *Benvenuto Cellini*, in 1838, which pleased

P.M. Chaperon's stage design for the premiere of Berlioz' "The Trojans" at the Théâtre Lyrique in Paris in 1863.
Bibliothèque de l'Opéra, Paris.

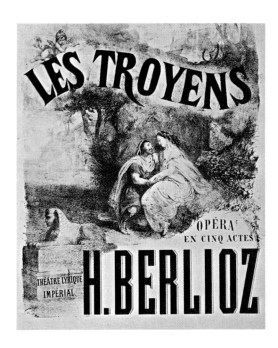

Poster advertising a performance of "The Trojans".
Bibliothèque de l'Opéra, Paris.

tunately, an unexpected gift arrived from someone who had heard the *Symphonie fantastique* and *Harold in Italy* with admiration. This was none other than Niccolò Paganini, who sent him the not inconsiderable sum of 20,000 francs. This allowed him to put his finances in order and return to composing. The result was *Roméo et Juliette*, a symphonic drama for soloists, chorus and orchestra (rather than a conventional opera, which would never have been accepted). It took a long time to compose, and was performed at the Paris Conservatory only in the winter of 1839. Success was immediate, however, partly making up for the earlier disaster of *Benvenuto Cellini*, and Berlioz subsequently accepted a commission to write recitatives for Weber's *Der Freischütz*. After the death of his wife, in 1842 he left on a long European tour which took him, among other places, to Leipzig, where he met Mendelssohn and Schumann. He travelled with a singer, Marie Geneviève Martin, with whom he had been in love for some time (she became his second wife in 1854, but died in 1862). The tour proved highly successful, and Berlioz' financial situation improved considerably as a result.

Berlioz wrote much during this period, and most of it is of great interest. The overture *Le carnaval romain* (The Roman Carnival), a lively reworking of themes from *Benvenuto Cellini*, came in 1843, and was followed in 1846 by the oratorio *La damnation*

neither the public nor the critics and proved Berlioz' worst disaster as a composer. From then on, the doors of opera houses were closed to him. He wished to continue composing, but he had a wife and a young child to support and lacked the financial security an artist needs to work properly. For-

On the right: Caricature of Berlioz on the first page of the Journal Amusant, 28th November, 1863. Bibliothèque de l'Opéra, Paris.
On the left: The devil flees in horror from a performance of "The Trojans" in a caricature by C.H. Champ. Cabinet des dessins, Louvre, Paris.

de Faust (The damnation of Faust) in which material from the earlier *Eight scenes from Faust*, inspired by his reading of Goethe was revised and reworked. Although the setting is now much broader, we again see Berlioz' tormented soul, as ever at odds with the rest of the world, projected in the figure of Faust. The Paris premiere on 6 December 1846 was not a success, however.

The spectacular *Te Deum* was completed in 1849, and the oratorio *L'enfance du Christ* (The childhood of Christ) was composed between 1850 and 1854. The transparency and clarity of the writing reflects Berlioz' reverential approach to the Latin texts from the Bible.

Then, with encouragement from Liszt, he began work on another opera. Turning to Virgil, a poet he loved, he spent the two years from 1856 to 1858 writing *Les Troyens* (The Trojans) which is in fact a double opera, each part based on two different sections of Virgil's epic. The first, *La prise de Troie* (The sacking of Troy) tells the story of the fall of the city, and was performed only after Berlioz' death in 1899. He was able, however, to see the second part, *Les Troyens à Carthage* (The Trojans in Carthage), based on the story of Dido and Aeneas.

His final compositions and writings are important since with hindsight they bring some sense of order to what otherwise seems a rather haphazard development as a composer. The important *Grand traité d'instrumentation et d'orchestration modernes* (Treatise on modern instrumentation and orchestration) was published in 1844, and was followed by *Les soirées de l'orchestre* (Orchestral evenings) in 1852 and *Les grotesques de la musique* (Musical grotesques) in 1859. His last opera, based appropriately enough on Shakespeare, was Béatrice et Bénédict of 1862.

After the death of his only child in 1867, Berlioz went on another long tour, this time to Germany and Russia. He died in Paris on 8 March 1869, a broken and lonely man, while preparing his *Memoirs* for publication.

It has often been said of Berlioz, and with some justice, that his life was nothing but love and the agonies of love. This may well be true, but it should be added that his restless imagination and desperate longings found their natural outlet and consummation in his masterly command of the orchestra. His music is scored for much larger orchestras than before, and new sonorities emerge from what are now regarded as his definitive groupings of instruments into permanent sections (strings, brass, winds, percussion, etc.) which have been used by composers ever since.

1910 poster advertising a performance of "The Damnation of Faust". Bibliothèque de l'Opéra, Paris.

Stage & vocal		
3 operas	Benvenuto Cellini	1834-38
	The Trojans (Part One: The Sack of Troy;	
	Part Two: The Trojans in Carthage)	1856-58
	Beatrice and Benedict	1860-62
other works for voices & orch.		
Sacred	including:	
	Resurrexit	1825
	Requiem (Grande messe des morts)	1837
	Te Deum	1849
	L'enfance du Christ	1850-54
Secular	including:	
	La morte d'Orphée	1827
	La révolution grecque	1826
	Eight scenes from 'Faust'	1826-29
	La mort de Cléopâtra	1829
	Lélio	1831
	Les nuits d'été	1834
	Romeo and Juliet	1839
	The Damnation of Faust	1846
	La mort d'Ophélie	1848

Orchestral		
6 overtures	Waverley	1827-28
	Les francs-juges	1827
	King Lear	1831
	Rob Roy	1832
	Carnaval romain	1843
	The Corsair	1850
1 symphony	Symphonie fantastique. Episodes in the	
	Life of an Artist	1829-30

Instrumental		
approx. 10	Harold in Italy for viola concertante & orch.	1834
misc. works	Rêverie et caprice for violin & orch.	1839

Songs		
approx. 30	including:	
songs	Hélène	1829
	La captive	1832
	La belle Isabeau	1844
	Le matin	1850

Chopin

Portrait of Frédéric Chopin. Watercolour by his friend Maria Wodzinska, 1826. National Museum, Warsaw.

Frédéric Chopin was born in Zelazowa Wola in Poland on 22 February 1810, but although Polish by birth and the son of a Pole, his spiritual home was always France. In fact it was never merely his adoptive country, because despite the fact that Chopin had long been considered the descendant of a Polish family that had moved to Paris, a number of documents prove his family came from the Loire region of France, and his father's birth certi-ficate states that he was born on 15 April 1771 in the village of Marainville near Nancy. He moved to Warsaw in 1787 where he married Tekla-Justyna Krzyzanowska on 2 June 1806. Frédéric was one of their four children.

Chopin had a comfortable upbringing. His father, an intelligent man, had quickly established himself as a French tutor in the richer households of the Polish capital. Later, again in Warsaw, he became a

French teacher in the lower school of the Lyceum. Now in a secure financial position, he converted his enormous apartment into a *pension* for pupils at the Lyceum, the majority of whom came from Poland's better families.

Chopin's personality was permanently moulded by the cultured, fashionable life of his home. An intelligent and attentive child, he soon felt that he was cut out to be a musician, and quickly proved it by his ability to play the piano (under guidance

farewell to his first teacher because, with his studies at the Lyceum over and a Rondo in C minor already published in 1825, he enroled in 1826 at the new Warsaw Conservatory, where he studied composition for the next three years under the perceptive guidance of Jozef K. Elsner. His masterly piano technique is evident in the compositions dating from this period, which include *Variations on a theme from Don Giovanni*, Op. 2, for piano and orchestra (1827), the Nocturne in E minor, Op. 72 no. 1

On the left: portrait of Jozef Ksawery Elsner, head of the Warsaw Conservatory. National Museum, Warsaw.

On the right: the salon at Chopin's home in Warsaw. Watercolour by Antoine Kolberg, 1832. L. Ciechomska collection.

from his sister) at the age of four. Later he was sent to a qualified Bohemian teacher for music tuition. His talent as a composer was soon evident. His first Polonaise in G minor of 1817, although not a great work, was an outstanding achievement for a child of seven, and he was mentioned in a Polish literary magazine in January 1818: 'We cannot pass over in silence the *Polonaise* for pianoforte by Frédéric Chopin, the seven-year-old son of Nicolas Chopin, a teacher of French language and literature'. After completing his piano studies and giving a series of concerts in aristocratic homes in and around Warsaw, he gave further proof of his exceptional composing talent in 1821 with another Polonaise, this time in A flat major, which he dedicated to his teacher. This was, in fact, a tactful way of saying

(1827), the Polonaise in D minor, Op. 71 no. 1 (1827), and the *Rondeau à la Mazur*, Op. 5 (1827).

In the meantime, Chopin was also making a name for himself as a concert pianist. Concluding his studies at the Conservatory in 1829, he embarked on a series of concerts that took him not only all over Poland but also to Vienna, where his extraordinary technique failed to make the impact it should have done because of the size of the concert halls there. However, he made a number of useful acquaintances who introduced him to the musical life of the city, including Schuppanzigh, who had played a major role in getting Beethoven's quartets known in Vienna, the publisher Haslinger who printed his *Variations*, Op. 2, in 1820, and Stein and Graff, the famous piano builders. He was also able

The Warsaw Conservatory where Chopin studied for three years under Elsner. National Museum, Warsaw.

to hear Rossini and Meyerbeer operas.

Returning to Warsaw in 1830, he played his First Piano Concerto in F minor, Op. 21 (1829) and Second Piano Concerto in E minor, Op. 11 (1830) at the National Theatre, but with little success. The press virtually ignored the event, although this is not surprising, perhaps, given the political situation at the time.

Chopin left Poland on 2 November 1830 for a study tour of Europe, perhaps with Italy as his final goal, but he could not have known then that he would never return to his beloved country. The first stop was Vienna, where he gave a single, rather unsuccessful concert. Then, with the shock waves of revolution spreading from France to Belgium, Italy and Poland, he decided that London would be the best place to live. On the way there, he learned that the Russian army had invaded Poland and suppressed the national government on 5 September 1831.

He was in Paris by the end of September, and although his ultimate aim was always to reach London, he decided to remain there, won over by the extraordinarily rich and stimulating musical life of the French capital. The cultured and refined young composer, who carried his pallid features and melancholy air extremely well, was immediately accepted by fashionable Paris. His first concert in the Salle Pleyel on 26 February 1832 included the First Piano Concerto, the *Variations on a theme of Mozart* and, among other shorter pieces, a *Grand Polonaise* for six pianos written by Kalkbrenner which was

The Salle Pleyel in Paris. Print. Archives de la Maison Pleyel, Paris.

performed on this occasion by the composer him-self, Mendelssohn, Chopin and other pianists. However, one of the critics present at the concert made disparaging comments about Chopin's play-ing, claiming that his touch was too light for con-certs in large halls. The result was that Chopin never won the recognition he deserved as a virtuo-so pianist, although he sometimes played in other concerts organised for charity or by other musi-cians.

He was fortunate to meet the Baron de Rothschild at one of these concerts. They quickly became friends, and the nobleman was able to open the doors of high Parisian society to the young compo-ser. Chopin's tuition was immediately requested and handsomely paid for, society hostesses compe-ted to have him in their salons, and his brilliant conversation captivated even the most sophisti-cated. At last he had found an audience that could appreciate him.

It also became easy to get his music published, in-cluding even the works he had written many years earlier. The three Nocturnes, Op. 9, written in Po-land between 1828 and 1830, the 12 Studies, Op. 10 (1829) dedicated to Liszt, and the Second Piano Concerto were all published in Paris during this period. The Studies, Op. 10, were particularly im-portant because, on a miniature scale, Chopin had extended the technical and expressive resources of the piano at a time when the instrument was going through a number of important changes, most no-tably the shift from wooden to metal frames, which enabled the action to be improved and gave the in-strument both a new range of tonal shading and the volume needed for large concert halls. The piano dominated the musical scene of Chopin's day, and he was the pianist of Paris's cultured élite, associa-ted through friendship with such famous names as Balzac, Heine, Liszt, and Ferdinand Hiller, with whom he travelled to Aix-la-Chapelle in May 1834.

Maurin, a group of the pianists of Chopin's time, including Liszt (seated, third from left) and Chopin (standing, third from left). Drawing. Gesellschaft der Musikfreunde, Vienna.

The following year saw him in Leipzig, where he met the Countess Maria Wodzinska to whom he would dedicate his gentle *Waltz in A flat major* (*L'a-dieu*) after their affair had ended. He also saw Mendelssohn again and met Clara and Robert Schumann who, with their usual enthusiasm, dubbed him Chopin the magnificent. Returning to Paris in December 1836, he met George Sand, the woman who changed the course of his life.

Cultured and refined as well as impulsive and temperamental, George Sand, the widow of Baron Dudevant, exerted an immediate influence on the young composer, and they remained together, in and out of love, until 1847, ten years in which Chopin attained his creative peak as a composer, producing such masterpieces as the third and fourth

Maria Wodzinska, pencil self-portrait. National Museum, Warsaw.

Portrait of George Sand by Auguste Charpentier. Cellule de Chopin collection, Palma, Majorca.

homes of Paris's social élite, but requests for lessons were not forthcoming and his health was deteriorating rapidly. His income was low and it was difficult to afford life in the French capital, which was becoming increasingly expensive because of social unrest. He decided to give a concert at the Salle Pleyel on 16 February 1848, but the effort weakened him considerably. He was ill, and as he confessed in a letter, '... I seem to be playing worse than ever'. Although composed largely of friends and admirers, the audience was quick to note the thinness of his tone. This was to be his last concert in France and, in effect, his farewell to Paris.

Having survived the violent insurrections of 1848, and with a slight improvement in his health, Chopin decided to leave Paris for London, partly on the insistence of one of his pupils. A concert on 20 April

George Sand in a satirical drawing on the emancipation of women. Musée Carnavalet, Paris.

Ballades (1841 and 1842), the Nocturnes, Op. 48 (1841-42), the three Polonaises, Opp. 44, 53 and 61 (1840-46), the Scherzo, Op. 54 (1843-44), the Fantasia in F minor, Op. 49 (1841) and the *Berceuse*, Op. 57 (1843).

With George Sand, in his retreat at Valdemosa on Majorca, he spent the winter of 1838 composing masterpieces which have justly taken their place alongside the other great works for piano. They include the second *Ballade*, Op. 38, dedicated to Schumann in 1840, the Mazurkas, Op. 33 and Op. 41, the Nocturnes, Op. 37, the Polonaises, Op. 40, and above all, the collection of 24 *Préludes*, Op. 28. After breaking with George Sand, Chopin mistakenly believed that he would be able to resume his comfortable, well paid life as a piano teacher in the

Tinted drawing by George Sand of the Villa "Son-Vent" in Palma, Majorca. Cellule de Chopin collection, Palma, Majorca.

1848 was a triumphant success, and he remained in Great Britain for seven months, giving a further nine concerts, the last of which, on 16 November, was organised to raise money for Polish refugees. However, Chopin was tired and weakened by travel, and the London climate disagreed with him. He left London on 23 November 1848 and returned to his beloved Paris, where he lived unhappily for a few years more. He had stopped composing, and had neither the strength nor the will to sit down at the keyboard. The instrument to which he had devoted the best part of his life no longer attracted him, and he had no further desire to run his fingers over its keys, although he may simply have been resigned to or overwhelmed by nostalgia for his native Poland.

He died in the early hours of the morning on 17 October 1849 in his home at Place Vendîme 12 in Paris, attended by his sister Louise and the Countess Potocka.

Piano		
16 polonaises	G minor	1817
	A flat major	1817
	A flat major	1821
	G sharp minor	1822-24
	B flat minor ('Adieu')	1826
	Three Polonaises Op. 71	1827-29
	G flat major	1830?
	Two Polonaises Op. 26	1834-35
	Two Polonaises Op. 40	1838-39
	F sharp minor	1840-41
	A flat major	1842
	Polonaise-Fantasia	1845-46
59 Mazurkas	B flat major (2 versions)	1825
	G major (2 versions)	1825
	D major	1829-30?
	Four Mazurkas Op. 6	1830
	Five Mazurkas Op. 7	1830
	Four Mazurkas Op. 68	1830-49
	Four Mazurkas Op. 24	1831?
	B flat major	1832
	D major (revised)	1832?
	Four Mazurkas Op. 17	1832-33?
	C major	1833?
	Four Mazurkas Op. 67	1835-49
	Four Mazurkas Op. 30	1836-37
	Four Mazurkas Op. 33	1837-38
	Four Mazurkas Op. 41	1838-39
	A minor	1840
	Three Mazurkas Op. 50	1841
	Three Mazurkas Op. 56	1843
	Three Mazurkas Op. 59	1845
	Three Mazurkas Op. 63	1846
	A flat major	?
	D major	-
	A minor (no. 2)	-
4 rondos	C minor	1825
	C major	1826-27
	Rondeau à la Mazur	1826
	E flat major	1832
21 nocturnes	C minor	1825c
	E minor	1827
	Three Nocturnes Op. 9	1828-30
	Three Nocturnes Op. 15	1830-33
	Two Nocturnes Op. 27	1834-35
	C sharp minor (lento con grande espressione)	before 1836
	Two Nocturnes Op. 32	1836-37
	Two Nocturnes Op. 37	1838-39
	Two Nocturnes Op. 48	1841-42
	Two Nocturnes Op. 55	1843-44
	Two Nocturnes Op. 62	1846?
3 sonatas	C minor	1828
	B flat minor	1836-39
	B minor	1844
18 waltzes	E major	1829
	Three Waltzes Op. 70	1829-41
	E minor	1830
	Grande valtzer brillante Op. 18	1831
	Three valtzer brillanti Op. 34	1831-38
	Two Waltzes Op. 69	1836
	Grande valtzer Op. 42	1840
	Three Waltzes Op. 64	1846-47
	A flat major	-
	E flat major	-
	A minor	-

27 studies	Twelve Studies Op. 10	1829
	Twelve Studies Op. 25	1830-34
	Three new Studies for the Moscheles method	pub. 1840
4 scherzos	B minor	1830?
	B flat minor	1837
	C sharp minor	1838-39
	E major	1842-43
4 impromptus	A flat major	1837
	F sharp major	1838
	G flat major	1842-43
	Fantasia-Impromptu Op. 66	1834?
4 ballades	G minor	1831
	F major	1838-39
	A flat major	1841
	F minor	1842
26 preludes	Twenty-Four Preludes Op. 28	1836-39
	A flat major	1834
	C sharp minor	1841
4 sets of variations	Variations on a German air	1824-25
	Variations on a theme by Paganini	1829?
	Introduction and Variations on a theme by Hérold	1833
	Variations on a theme by Bellini	1834
other works	Contraddanza	1827?
	Funeral march (2 versions)	1829
	Three Scottish dances Op. 72. 3-5	1830c
	Allegro da concerto	1831-32
	Bolero	1833
	Largo	1833-36
	Cantabile	1834
	Tarantella	1841
	Fantasia in F minor	1841
	Two-Part Fugue	1841?
	Berceuse	1843
	Feuille d'album	1845-46

Concertos		
2 piano concertos	F minor	1829
	E minor	1830
other works for piano & orch.	Variations on theme from Mozart's 'Don Giovanni'	1827
	Fantasia on Polish airs	1828
	Krakowiak	1828
	Andante spianato and Grand Polonaise Brillant	1831-32

Songs		
20 songs with piano accompaniment	The Spell	1829-30
	Seventeen Polish songs	1829-47
	Dumka	1840

Mendelssohn

Portrait of Felix Mendelssohn Bartholdy. Mendelssohn Archive, Berlin.

When European Romanticism was at its height, Felix Mendelssohn lived his brief life in an atmosphere of orderly calm, far removed from the stormy passions and controversies that raged about him, composing exquisitely crafted music of the highest artistic merit. Born in Hamburg in 1809 into a Jewish family of prosperous bankers and intellectuals, he had a secure, affluent upbringing and a father who immediately provided everything necessary for a first-class private education (being Jewish, Felix was not allowed to attend state schools). His brilliant intelligence was nurtured and encouraged by private tutors in Berlin, where the family had moved in 1811, and he received a solid grounding in the subjects that were to provide the basis for his first-rate liberal and Humanistic education. He studied literature and tried his hand at painting (some of his delicate watercolours

The opulent Mendelssohn home in Berlin. Drawing. Mendelssohn Archive, Berlin.

The young Mendelssohn at the piano around 1820.

have survived), but his greatest passion was music. Mendelssohn's father Abraham, and mother Lea Bartholdy, an intelligent and cultivated woman, encouraged their son in his early musical interests, and later sent him for further study to the pianist Friedrich Zelter, an excellent teacher who quickly perceived the exceptional musical gifts of his brilliant pupil. Under his expert guidance, Felix made excellent progress and strove to better the achievement of his sister Fanny who was also an extraordinarily gifted musician. His first public concert on 24 October 1818 at the age of nine brought him immediate success as a child prodigy, a second Mozart, but he remained unaffected by it, continuing his orderly life of study in the comfort of his beautiful home and secure in the love of his parents and family.

Obviously, it was the wealth of the Mendelssohn family that made possible the kind of systematic, well rounded education their gifted son received, and there can be little doubt that his ardent, sensitive nature found all the encouragement it needed within the cultured circle of his father's friends who met every Sunday to 'make music' in his luxurious Berlin home.

94

When still very young Felix was also fortunate to be introduced by his teacher Zelter to the great poet Goethe at Weimar in November 1821. The meeting between the revered old man and the 12-year-old boy went extremely well. 'He is an exquisite, divine youth,' Goethe wrote to Felix's parents. 'Nothing is more comforting than to see budding young talents like him who promise to go far.'

And in fact, Mendelssohn was already well on the way to fame. He began composing in 1820: a small set of one-movement violin sonatas, some string quartets, some songs and some sacred choruses. It can be said that by 1820 he was already a mature composer and man.

A contemporary of Chopin (b. 1810), Schumann (b. 1810) and Liszt (b. 1811), Mendelssohn developed his musical talent very early and had become an established part of the European musical scene a good ten years before his other great contempora-

ded after consulting his friend Ignaz Moscheles, the famous concert pianist, who happened to be in Berlin at the time, he went to Paris to seek the advice of the Italian composer Cherubini. Both musicians could do no other than acknowledge the exceptional musical gifts of his young son.

Two years later, in 1826, the 17-year-old composer's genius again astounded the world, this time with the incidental music for Shakespeare's *A midsummer night's dream*, one of Mendelssohn's greatest orchestral scores, which goes straight to the imaginative heart of Shakespeare's comedy. The same dreamlike atmosphere would later pervade his famous *Eight songs without words* for piano – delicate works of consummate poetic refinement.

After studying history and philosophy (under Hegel) at Berlin University, Mendelssohn was a more than usually well-educated young man, and certainly more cultured than any other musician of his

The young Mendelssohn plays the piano for Goethe. Staatliche Kunstsammlungen Schlossmuseum, Weimar.

ries. His First Symphony of 1824 was followed in 1825 by a minor masterpiece, the Octet, Op. 20, an exquisite combination of refined elegance and youthful energy.

Although the First Symphony was a success, the young composer's father was unsure whether his son ought even to think of attempting to make a career in the difficult world of music. Still undeci-

time. When we add to this the journeys to France, Great Britain and Switzerland which his father's wealth enabled him to make in lordly style, it is easy to see how he assimilated the art and culture of the ancient and modern worlds as if it were his natural right and inheritance. More specifically, the music of the past became not so much a passion in him as a kind of worship or cult, an unqualified

Below: Piazza di Spagna, Rome, in a drawing by Mendelssohn produced during his Italian tour. Mendelssohn Archive, Berlin.

On the right: Durham Cathedral in a watercolour by Mendelssohn. Mendelssohn Archive, Berlin.

admiration for the incomparable formal perfection and poise of certain Classical and Baroque masterpieces.

This alone explains the almost religious ardour with which, at only 20 years old, the composer conducted the first performance in modern times of Bach's *St Matthew passion* at the Berlin Singakademie on 10 March 1829, an achievement which alone would have assured him a permanent place in the history of European music. The performance was a resounding success and initiated a general revival of interest in the music of J.S. Bach and other Baroque composers.

1829 saw Mendelssohn's first visit to Great Britain, whose cultural similarities with Germany coupled with his own natural disposition made him regard it as his second country. He lived happily in London, gave many concerts (waiving the usual fee), met the leading musical figures of his day and made a name for himself as an exceptional pianist and conductor. A journey to Scotland and the Hebrides produced the famous overture *Die Hebriden* (The Hebrides), Op. 26, also known as *Fingal's cave*, perhaps one of the most successful of all German

Romantic compositions.

Returning home briefly, the young composer soon set off on his travels once again. Travelling featured largely in his short life, partly because his father's wealth made it possible but also because his natural restlessness and constant desire to discover new people and things made it necessary to him. He visited Goethe in Weimar in May 1830, the last time they were ever to meet. A reading of one of Goethe's poems inspired *Die erst Walpurgisnacht*, a cantata for chorus and orchestra. The next stop, after a brief stay in Munich, was Vienna, where a whole month's visit left virtually no impression on Mendelssohn at all because he could find no pianist able or willing to play Beethoven for him.

Finally, in October 1830, he crossed the Alps into Italy. 'Here I am in Italy,' he wrote. 'I've always looked forward to this as one of the greatest joys of my life.' A fervid admirer of Goethe and his 'Journey to Italy', Mendelssohn went off in enthusiastic pursuit of the artistic treasures of ancient and Renaissance Italy, and above all, its glorious painting. His main love was Italian art, and he was fascinated by the ruins of the ancient world, but Italian musical life seemed to interest him rather less, perhaps because he was already a mature composer fully aware of his capabilities before he ever came to Italy (his haughty detachment from the Italian musical world was as much a part of his character as anything else). He was captivated, however, by the colourful street life, natural beauty, agreeable climate and wonderful art treasures of Rome. 'The whole of Rome stands before me so that I may enjoy it,' he writes in one letter. 'Every impression becomes deep and unforgettable to me.'

His stay in Italy lasted ten months, during which time Mendelssohn visited Venice, Florence, Rome, Naples, Pompeii and Milan. He worked on *Die erst Walpurgisnacht*, *Fingal's cave*, the concerto, Op. 25 and the *Scottish Symphony*, and started sketching the Fourth Symphony *Italian* in A major.

Leaving Italy, Mendelssohn began his journey home, but his wanderings had not yet ended. Having crossed Switzerland, he stopped in Paris and then returned once again to Great Britain, where he remained in London from April to June

Above: title-page of Mendelssohn's overture to "A Midsummer Night's Dream". Tate Gallery, London.
Below: View of Lucerne. Watercolour by Mendelssohn. Mendelssohn Archive, Berlin.

Portrait of Cécile Mendelssohn, wife of the composer. Mendelssohn Archive, Berlin.

Portrait of Mendelssohn's daughter Lilli and son Carl painted by their mother. Mendelssohn Archive, Berlin.

1832. His second visit to the British capital was a triumph. Mendelssohn gave concerts with his pianist friend Moscheles, played Mozart's Concerto for two pianos with him, gave organ recitals in St Paul's Cathedral and had his first collection of *Songs without words* printed. *Fingal's cave*, the Concerto, Op. 25 and the overture to *A midsummer night's dream* became popular and successful everywhere.

Mendelssohn was aware of a change in himself when he returned to Germany. Music was now no longer a matter of instinctive pleasure or amateur indulgence but a serious profession. Bitter disappointment was also waiting for him there. He may well have cherished the dream of succeeding his old teacher Zelter, who had died in 1832, as director of the Berlin Singakademie, but he was passed over, perhaps because of his Jewish origins, although he had been a Protestant convert for some time. Thus, he willingly accepted the post of ***Musikdirektor*** in Düsseldorf, and further consolidated his career by becoming director of the Leipzig Gewandhaus. This was the city of Bach, the cradle of German music, the city which would offer free rein to his talents and ambitions, and he never left it. There he established his home with his wife Cécile whom he had married on 28 March 1837, and brought up his five children. He also worked extremely hard. In only a few years he had reorganised

the Gewandhaus Orchestra, founded the Conservatory where he himself taught piano and composition, and transformed concert programmes to include works that were particularly dear to him. The symphony-cantata *Lobegesang* (Hymn of praise) was written in 1840 for performance before the monument to Gutenberg, and he gave an organ recital in the Church of St Thomas on 6 August 1840 to raise the money needed for a monument to Bach. Mendelssohn, deeply shocked by the sudden death of his father in 1835, devoted himself even more intensely to his work, completing the oratorio *Paulus* in only a few months. He travelled again, returning to London and directing five festivals in Cologne, Düsseldorf and Braunschweig. He was called to Berlin by Wilhelm Frederick IV in 1841, and after a stay in Frankfurt returned again to Leipzig. Still a young man, he spent his final years exhausted by over-work and afflicted by family tragedies which gradually weakened his delicate sensibility. His mother died in 1842, followed by his sister Fanny on 17 May 1847. Mendelssohn was inconsolable and, closing himself in his grief, virtually never composed again. He died peacefully in Leipzig on 4 November in the same year, leaving the oratorio *Christus* unfinished.

Although attracted to Romanticism and susceptible to its effects, Mendelssohn was never able to commit himself to it emotionally. He was an important figure in the musical world of his time, a respected composer of poised, elegant music. The quantity and quality of his output was outstanding, given the brevity of his life. In addition to his early symphonies, the later Symphony No. 4 *Italian*, Symphony No. 3 *Scottish* and Symphony No. 5 *Reformation* are now part of the standard orchestral repertoire. His concertos include the wonderful Violin Concerto in E minor, Op. 64. Of his sacred music, the oratorios *Paulus* and *Elias* (which many consider a masterpiece) are particularly fine.

The Gewandhaus, Leipzig, in a 19th-century print. Wagner Gedenkstätte, Bayreuth.

Stage		
7 operas (1 unfinished)	Die beiden Pädagogen (The Two Teachers)	1820
	Die Soldatenliebschaft (Comradely Love)	1820
	Die wanderenden Komödianten (The Strolling Players)	1820
	Die beiden Neffen (The Two Nephews)	1822
	Die Hochzeit des Camacho (Camacho's Wedding)	1827
	Die Heimkehr aus der Fremde	1829
	Loreley (unfinished)	1847
5 sets of incidental music	including:	
	Antigone (Sophocles)	1841
	A Midsummer Night's Dream (Shakespeare)	1843
	Athalie (Racine)	1845
	Oedipus at Colonus (Sophocles)	1845

Vocal		

Sacred

3 oratorios (1 unfinished)	Paulus	1836
	Elijah	1846
	Christus (unfinished)	1847
35 works with accompaniment	including	
	5 canatas	1830-32
	3 motets	1830
	5 Psalms	1830-43
	Drei geistliche Lieder	-
	Zwei geistliche Lieder (post.)	1876
29 chamber works	including:	
	Three Psalms for 8 voices	1843-44
	Sechs Sprüche for doublechorus	1844-46
	German Lithurgy for 8 voices (3 pieces)	1846
	Three motets for the English Church for soloists, and four-part choir	1847

Secular

6 works with accompaniment	including:	
	Die erste Walpurgisnacht	1830
	Festgesang	1840
approx. 50 chamber works	including:	
	Six male choruses	1837-40
	Four choruses	1837-44

Symphonies		
17 symphonies	12 symphonies for strings	1820-24
	Symphony No. 1 in C minor	1824
	Symphony No. 5 in D minor ('Reformation')	1830
	Symphony No. 4 in A major ('Italian')	1833
	Symphony No. 2 in B flat major ('Lobgesang') for soloists, chorus, organ and orchestra	1840
	Symphony No. 3 in A minor ('Scottish')	1842
9 overtures	including:	
	A Midsummer Night's Dream	1826
	Calm Sea and Prosperous Voyage	1828-32
	The Hebrides (Fingal's Cave)	1829
	The Fair Melusine	1833

Concertos		
3 piano concertos	Concerto in A minor	1823-24
	Concerto No. 1 in G minor	1831
	Concerto No. 2 in D minor	1837
2 violin concertos	Concerto in D minor	1822
	Concerto In E minor	1844
2 concertos for two pianos	Concerto in E major	1823
	Concerto in A flat major	1824
also	Concerto for piano, violin and strings	1823
	Capriccio brillante for piano and orch.	1826
	Rondo brillante for piano and orch.	1834
	Serenade & Allegro goioso for piano & orch.	1838

Chamber		
1 octet	Octet in E flat major	1825
1 sextet	Sextet in D major for piano, oboe & strings	1824
2 string quintets	Quintet No. 1 in A major	1831
	Quintet No. 2 in B major	1845
7 string quartets	Quartet in E flat major	1823
	Quartet No. 1 in E flat major	1828
	Quartet No.2 in A minor	1829
	Quartet No. 3 in D minor	1837-38
	Quartet No. 4 in E minor	1837-38
	Quartet No. 5 in E flat major	1837-38
	Quartet No. 6 in F minor	1837-38
3 piano quartets	Piano Quartet No. 1 in C minor	1822
	Piano Quartet No. 2 in F minor	1823
	Piano Quartet No. 3 in B minor	1824-25
3 piano trios	Trio in C minor	1820
	Trio No. 1 in D minor	1839
	Trio No. 2 in C minor	1845
sonatas for instruments and piano	2 Violin Sonatas	1823-38
	1 Viola Sonata	1824
	1 Clarinet Sonata	1824
	2 Cello Sonatas	1838-43
also	Variations concertantes for cello & piano	1829
	2 Concert Pieces for basset horn & piano	1833

Piano		
16 collections	Seven Characteristic Pieces	1827
	Six Preludes and Fugues	1827-37
	Three Fantasias or Caprices	1829
	8 Books of Songs Without Words (6 pieces per Book)	1829-45
	Three Caprices	1833-35
	Three Studies	1834-38
	Three Preludes	1836
	Six Pieces for Children	1842-43
	Two Pieces for Children	(pub.) 1860
3 sonatas	Sonata in G minor	1821
	Sonata in E major	1826
	Sonata in E flat major	1827
3 sets of variations	Variations sérieuses in D minor	1841
	Variations in E flat major	1841
	Variations in B flat major	1841
13 other works	including:	
	Prelude and Fugue	1841
	Perpetuum mobile	(pub.) 1873
4 pieces for piano duet	including:	
	Allegro brillante	1841
	Duo concertante	

Organ		
36 works	including:	
	23 Preludes and Fugues	1822-37
	Three Preludes and Fugues	1837
	Six Organ Sonatas	1839-45
	Fugue in F minor	1839
	Praeludium in C minor	1841
	2 Organ Pieces	1844

Songs		
approx. 100 works	including:	
	2 sets of 12 songs	1825-28
	7 sets of 6 songs	1826-47
	1 set of 3 songs	1831-34
	1 set of 2 songs	1835
	Two romances	1833-34
	Three duets	1836-47
	Six duets	1842-44
	The Garland	1829
	Seemans Scheidelied	1831
	Das Mädchens Klage	1835?
	Warnung von dem Rhein	-
	Lied (from Ruy Blas)	-
	Todeslied der Bojaren	-

Schumann

Portrait of the young Schumann. Schumannhaus, Zwickau.

Spiritual heir to Bach and Beethoven, precursor of Chopin and Brahms, a shrewd and committed critic and an aristocratic intellectual open to any kind of engagement with poetry and literature, Robert Schumann embodied in musical form the intellectual and emotional ebb and flow of the whole German Romantic movement. He was born at Zwickau in Saxony on 8 June 1810, the last of five children. His father, a bookseller and publisher, loved literature and music. His mother, a gifted amateur musician, gave him a certain amount of piano tuition, and by the age of 11 he had already tried to give his adolescent dreams concrete form in a short composition for voices and instruments based on the 150th psalm.

He read extremely widely, but the writer who had, as Schumann himself put it, an 'ecstatic' effect on him was Friedrich Richter, the recently (1825) deceased German author who had adopted the French pseudonym of Jean Paul Richter. Although he adored music, Schumann was enrolled in the Faculty of Jurisprudence at Leipzig University in 1828. He raised no objection, but fell into a state of profound apathy. Once over the first shock, howe-

Portrait of Dr. Carl Erdmann Carus, whose wife was a friend of Schumann's. Schumannhaus, Zwickau.

ver, he made an effort to fit in. He went to **salles d'armes**, explored the countryside around Leipzig, travelled to Munich and Bayreuth with his friend Rosen, began to study the philosophy of Kant, Fichte, Schelling and Hegel, took fencing lessons, played the piano, and wrote exquisite letters of Proustian intimacy.

The arrival in Leipzig of Doctor Carus, an old Zwickau acquaintance, terminated this uneasy, directionless period in his life. Welcomed into a friendly home, Schumann at last felt that he could relax and speak openly, uninhibited by the painful shyness he had always felt in the presence of strangers. Carus' friends included an unusual couple, a Professor Wieck and his daughter, who were also master and pupil. Clara Wieck, to whom Schumann was to be bound for the rest of his life, was an exceptional girl with an innate talent for music (she was already a successful concert pianist at less than ten years of age).

Schumann and Wieck understood each other immediately, and their master-pupil relationship could not have been happier nor more cordial. Under Wieck's strict though perceptive guidance, he consolidated a piano technique that until then had been rather patchy, and although his musical studies occupied most of his time, he continued reading law in order to please his mother.

Towards the end of August 1829 Schumann set off for Italy and returned two months later after visiting Brescia, Milan and Venice. Having moved

from Leipzig to Heidelberg, he again felt restless. His complex, shifting nature yearned incessantly for love, beauty and music, and the crisis that had been building up in him for some time suddenly came into the open at an Easter concert in Frankfurt on 11 April 1830, when he heard Paganini play for the first time. The experience was a dazzling revelation to him, as if Paganini had unveiled an ancient, hidden truth in him. By the summer of 1830 he had understood the magical power of music for the first time.

With his mother's encouragement and Wieck's approval, Schumann used the portion of the family capital that had fallen to him upon his coming of age to concentrate more fully on his musical studies. 1831 was an important year in his musical life. As he refined his critical taste in the cultivated musical atmosphere of Leipzig, he unknowingly prepared himself for what would become his second major artistic and professional vocation in life, that of the music critic. With its music societies, Gewandhaus concerts, the Academy, and its many virtuoso chamber ensembles, Leipzig was one of the musical capitals of Schumann's day. Musical information there came from direct experience of music; new scores were continually being played and discussed. Schumann's first article was published in the December issue of a new musical re-

The Gewandhaus, Leipzig, in a 19th-century watercolour.

Portrait of Paganini in a miniature by Paul de Pommayrac. Palazzo Doria Tursi, Genoa.

view called *Allegemeine Musikalische Zeitung* (Universal musical gazette). The event was of some importance, for Schumann, with the acute critical insight that distinguished all his later writings, introduced to the musical world of Leipzig a musician who until then had been completely ignored, Frédéric Chopin, saying in effect: 'Remove your hats, ladies and gentlemen; this man is a genius'. And yet, Schumann could well have said the same about himself. The 'creative potential' he had only vaguely been aware of previously now began to take on concrete form. His musical sketches became more coherent, more polished, and a piano concerto, various symphonic movements, and above all, piano pieces began to take shape. At last, in 1831, his first work was published, the *Theme and Variations on the name Abegg*, Op. 1, for piano. He also wrote *Papillons*, Op. 2, for piano in this period, although it was published the following year in 1832. Framed by two dance episodes, the 12 pieces that make up *Papillons* already confirm his genius as a composer. The sequence of sometimes extremely short musical fragments shows his brilliance in creating an atmosphere or portraying a state of mind, using the briefest possible musical means. Early in 1832, as he went ahead with, as he put it, the 'desperate and demented' course of self-imposed study that kept him daily for hours at the keyboard, Schumann strained the fourth finger of his right hand, which stiffened and subsequently paralysed the whole hand. In spite of homoeopathic

therapy, he never fully recovered the use of his right hand, and was obliged to abandon his career as a concert pianist. Now that he was no longer playing the piano, his rate of composition naturally increased, and by 1833 he had produced a significant number of important works. The *Studies on caprices by Paganini*, Op. 3, and the *Six concert studies on caprices by Paganini*, Op. 10, are both his homage to the Italian violinist who had opened his eyes to the mysterious power of music, as well as a recreation in pianistic terms of the violin virtuosity he had heard from Paganini. Virtuosity is also a prominent feature of other less important pieces of this period such as the *Six intermezzi*, Op. 4, and the Impromptu, Op. 54, on a theme by Clara Wieck, but it acquires a new significance in the splendid Toccata, Op. 7, an undeniably great composition even if *Papillons* remains his masterpiece of this period. The driest technical procedures are transformed by Schumann into a crystalline flow of brilliant music, a *moto perpetuo* of colour and rhythm.

The October of 1833 was darkened by the sudden deaths at an early age of both his own brother Julian, and the wife of Carl, another of his brothers. Schumann was deeply shocked, and withdrew into deep depression, a first sign of the madness

Poster advertising a concert in Zwickau on 18 November 1832 in which Schumann first appeared as a composer. Schumannhaus, Zwickau.

103

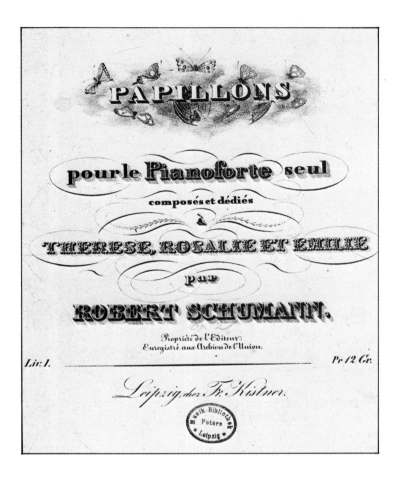

Title-page of Schumann's "Papillons", Op. 2. Peters music library, Leipzig.

that destroyed him in later life. The attack of depression impeded the creative flow of his composition, but he continued to work nonetheless.

The work that cost Schumann the greatest emotional effort, in the sense that it was composed in a mental state that oscillated between euphoric optimism and the deepest depression, was the *Grande Sonata* in F sharp minor, Op. 11, which he completed in 1835. It was followed later in 1835 by perhaps his greatest piano work, *Carnaval*, Op. 9, a collection of 20 short pieces 'on four notes'.

Feeling the need to compose on a larger scale, Schumann returned to the sonata form and produced the great *Phantasie*, Op. 17, which is in fact a sonata in spite of its name, although full of Schumannesque 'fantasy' elements. The *Phantasie* is a mature work in which Schumann handles large architectural structures with a fluency and ease he rarely achieved in later works.

However, he had other interests beside composing. His brilliant debut as a music critic has already been mentioned, and this early promise was only confirmed by his later writings. A circle of avant-garde musicians and writers gradually formed around him. Their lively meetings in a tavern in the Fleichergasse were occasions for heated discussion in which the works of Beethoven, Bach, Weber and Schubert were exalted, and the efforts of new musicians, especially Chopin and Mendelssohn, were seen as representative of a typically German musical originality which official critics had ignored for too long. A new league was formed which was, as Schumann said, 'more than secret because it existed only in the brain of its founder', the 'League of the Brothers of David' that would do battle against bourgeois prejudice and musical Philistinism in the name of progress and free Romantic inspiration.

With the death of his closest friend, Schunke, and the indifference of Hartmann, the owner of the magazine Schumann was writing for, the *Neue Zeitschrift für Musik*, the ideals of the League seemed doomed to failure, but Schumann took upon himself all the publishing and editing duties of the magazine, and it became, in effect, his own creation (his name has always been associated with it in music criticism since then). Although youthful and enthusiastic in tone, the magazine was also remarkable for the high level of debate it offered and the clarity of its intellectual and theoretical stance, and it quickly became one of the leading musical periodicals of its day.

The early creative period dominated almost entire-

Portrait of Friedrich Wieck, the father of Clara Schumann and a famous piano teacher. Schumannhaus, Zwickau.

The young Clara Schumann at the piano. Lithograph, 1835. Civica Raccolta di Stampe Bertarelli, Milan.

the capitals of Europe, hoping that the long separation involved would weaken her attachment to Schumann.

Clara came of age in 1840 and so was free to marry without the consent of her father. Much against their will, the couple went to law, and the Leipzig Royal Court of Appeal authorised their marriage, which took place on 12 September 1840. Wieck, unrelenting, did not attend the wedding.

Their marriage was a happy one, both artistically and emotionally. In the months before his wedding Schumann wrote a series of songs which undoubtedly represent the peak of his creative life. As a song writer he continued the great tradition established by Schubert, although he never quite achieved Schubert's rapt intensity of vision. This may be because Schubert had a more instinctive genius for sung melody and the possibilities of the voice, and a less oblique expressive idiom, but Schumann's extraordinary expressive power and psychological insight at least match and in some cases surpass those of Schubert. Also, the piano is given a new role in Schumann's songs: paradoxically, perhaps, it could almost be said that his writing for piano achieves its greatest subtlety and originality in the

Schumann's favourite corner in the Kaffeebaum in a drawing by Kienmayer. Schumannhaus, Zwickau.

ly by the piano came to an end around 1838-39 with an impressive series of important compositions, even though the composer's most original piano works had already been written by then: *Kriesleriana*, Op. 16, a collection of pieces based on Hoffmann's fictitious **Kapellmeister** Kriesler ranging from the grotesque to the sublime; the eight *Novelletten*, Op. 21; the Sonata in G minor, Op. 22; *Kinderscenen* (Scenes from childhood), Op. 15, a masterpiece of psychological insight; and the kaleidoscopic *Humoresque*, Op. 20.

After innumerable difficulties, Schumann married Clara Wieck in 1840 when he was at the height of his artistic powers. As a young girl, Clara had always been present at the League's lively meetings, and had quickly become, in effect, the inspirational force behind it with her charm and acute artistic sensibility, but when Schumann approached her father in 1836 he refused to allow them to marry on account of his daughter's youth and, above all, Schumann's uncertain financial position as a musician and his poor health. To make matters worse, he sent Clara away on a gruelling concert tour of

Clara and Robert Schumann in 1847. Schumannhaus, Zwickau.
Six of Clara and Robert Schumann's eight children. Schumannhaus, Zwickau.

accompaniments to his songs, where his innate pianism is challenged to its utmost by the poetic qualities of the texts of the songs. Thus, we have *Liederkreise*, Op. 24, based on poems by Heine; the *Myrthen* cycle, Op. 25, based on text by Goethe, Rückert, Byron, Heine and others; *Liederkriese*, Op. 39, based on poems by Eichendorff; the beautiful *Frauenliebe und -leben cycle* (The life and love of a woman), Op. 42, based on a text by Adelbert von Chamisso, perhaps his greatest song masterpiece; and finally, the *Diechterliebe* (Love of a poet), Op. 48, based again on poems by Heine.

The gradual slide into madness of Schumann the man is countered in his music by a slow distancing from the unstable though fully authentic fantasies of his youth towards an apparent, though relatively uninspired, mental calm and balance.

In the field of chamber music, the three String Quartets, Op. 42 (1842) are particularly fine, especially the one in A major, and the piano contributes a subtle brilliance to the Quintet, Op. 47 (1842) and

Trio, Op. 63 (1847). The two Violin Sonatas, Op. 105 (1851) and Op. 121 (1851), although perhaps less consistent, have moments of extraordinary emotional insight and power.

Schumann's four symphonies, though structurally weak, are impressive musically and, with their original orchestration, have remained central to the German symphonic tradition. The Piano Concerto, Op. 54 (1846), the *Introduction and Allegro*, Op. 92 (1849) for piano and orchestra and the Cello Concerto, Op. 129 (1850) are also popular because they have an attractive, 'improvised' feel in performance.

Genoveva, Op. 81 (1847), Schumann's only opera, has never recovered from its disastrous first performance in 1850 (although it should be remembered that it appeared in the same year as Wagner's *Lohengrin*) and perhaps merits reconsideration precisely because of its Wagnerian elements. His three non-religious oratorios, *Das Paradies und die Peri* (Paradise and the Peri), Op. 50 (1843), *Scenes* from Goethe's *Faust* (1847-53) and the fable *Der Rose Pilgerfahrt* (The pilgrimage of the rose), Op. 112 (1851) are more successful, and are related to the choral symphony *Requiem für Mignon*, Op. 98b (1849) with its typically Schumannesque lyrical tension.

Although Schumann continued to compose, something seemed to be crumbling in his personality. Clara had made triumphant concert appearances abroad in Copenhagen, Hamburg and Bohemia, and the couple were lionised socially and artistically during their visit to Russia, but Schumann was increasingly uneasy. In 1844 he had to give up his piano and composition teaching at the Leipzig Conservatory (which Mendelssohn had founded), and his doctors advised him to move to another city. Suffering now from amnesia and circulatory problems, obsessed by a fear of violent death and prey to violent fluctuations of mood, he moved to Dresden in 1846, where he suffered further collapse that produced another furious burst of composing. Moving from Dresden to Düsseldorf in 1850,

he accepted the post of music director in the city, but was forced to resign because of increasing mental instability. His last article as critic appeared in 1853. In it, he pointed with characteristic insight to the greatness of the young Johannes Brahms (whom he had just met), regarding him as the true successor to Beethoven in the field of symphonic music, a distinction he himself had always been denied.

When he returned to Düsseldorf from a visit to Holland Schumann was virtually at the end of his resources, racked by insomnia because afraid of dying in his sleep. Convinced that he was being pursued, he fled from his house on a freezing night in February 1854 and threw himself into the Rhine. He was rescued by boatmen and taken home, but his madness was by now almost total. He was taken to a clinic at Endenich near Bonn, and was refused visitors. He died on 29 July 1856.

Clara lived for many years after and was instrumental in establishing the greatness of her husband's music throughout the world.

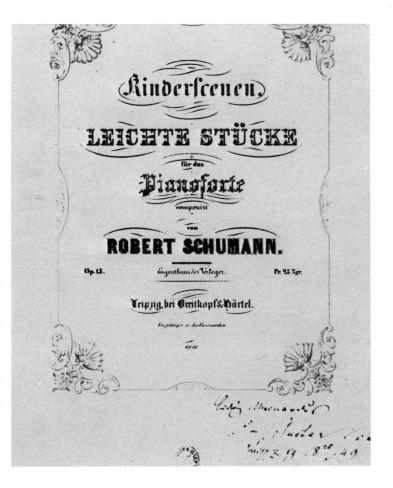

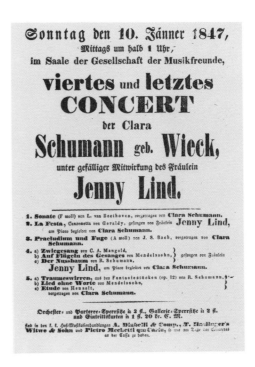

Title-page of Schumann's "Kinderscenen" (Scenes from Childhood). Schumannhaus, Zwickau.

Poster advertising a concert by Clara Schumann and Jenny Lind in Vienna in 1847. Schumannhaus, Zwickau.

Stage		
2 operas	Il Corsaro (The Corsair) (unfinished)	1844
	Genoveva	1847
incidental music	Manfred	1848

Songs		
approx. 300 songs for voice & piano	including:	
	Liederkreis (9 songs)	1840
	Myrthen (26 songs)	1840
	Frauenliebe und -leben (8 songs)	1840
	Dichterliebe (16 songs)	1840
	Gedichte der Königin Maria Stuart (5 songs)	1852

Vocal		
approx. 100 choral works	including:	
	Das Paradies und die Peri (oratorio)	1841-43
	Requiem für Mignon (oratorio)	1849
	The Pilgrimage of the Rose (approx. 80 pieces for chamber choir)	1840-50
1 canon	Hirtengesang	1846

Piano		
more than 250 pieces for solo piano	including:	
	Papillons	1829-32
	Theme and Variations on the name ABEGG	1830
	Carnaval (20 pieces)	1834-35
	Davidsbündlertänze (18 pieces)	1837
	Phantasiestücke (8 pieces)	1837
	Scenes from Childhood (13 pieces)	1838
	Kriesleriana (8 fantasias)	1838
	Novelletten (8 pieces)	1838
	Klavierstücke (4 pieces)	1838-39
	Album for the Young (43 pieces)	1848
	Forest Scene (9 pieces)	1848-49
43 pieces for piano duet 2 pianos	including:	
	12 piano pieces for children young and old	1849
	Anante and Variations in B flat major	1843

Organ		
17 pieces	including:	
	Six Fugues on the name "BACH"	1845

Orchestral		
6 symphonies	Symphony in G minor (unfinished)	1832
	Symphony No. 1 in B flat major ("Spring")	1841
	Symphony in C minor (unfinished)	1841
	Symphony No. 2 in C major	1846
	Symphony No. 3 in E flat major ("Rhenish")	1850
	Symphony No. 4 in D minor	1851
6 overtures	including:	
	Overture, Scherzo & Finale in E major	1841
	Overture to Hermann und Dorothea (Goethe)	1851

Instrumental		
4 piano concertos (3 unfinished)	including: Piano concerto in A major	1841-45
3 other works piano & orch.	including: Konzertstück in G major	1849
1 cello concerto	Cello concerto in A minor	1850
1 violin concerto	Violin concerto in D minor (post)	1853
1 concerto for 4 horns	Konzertstück in F major	1849

Chamber		
6 quartets	including: Quartet Op. 47 for strings and piano	1842
1 quintet for strings & piano	Quintet in E flat major	1842
3 piano trios	Trio in D minor	1847
	Trio in F major	1847
	Trio in G minor	1851
2 violin sonatas	Sonata in A minor	1851
	Sonata in D minor	1851
other works	including: Phantasiestücke for violin, cello & piano	1852

Verdi

Portrait of Giuseppe Verdi by Giovanni Boldini. Casa di Riposo Giuseppe Verdi, Milan.

Giuseppe Verdi, the son of Luigia Uttini and Carlo Verdi, was born in 1813 at Roncole di Busseto, a small village near Parma in northern Italy. His birth certificate is one of the last official documents written in French in Busseto. The village was then still in the Dukedom of Parma, and so belonged to one of the transalpine *Départements* Napoleon administered directly from France after conquering much

of an Italy still divided into small city-states. The Napoleonic Empire collapsed after the horrendous retreat of the French army from Moscow in the terrible Russian winter of 1812-13, and only a few days after Verdi's birth, the battle of Leipzig once more placed northern Italy under Austrian control. As a result, the Dukedom of Parma, Piacenza and Guastalla was reconstituted, and was governed from 1815

The fortress at Busseto in a 19th-century painting. Museo Civico, Busseto.

on by Marie Louise, Grand-Duchess of Austria and wife of Napoleon.

Giuseppe's first teacher was a local priest, Don Pietro Baistrocchi, an infant school teacher and organist whose death in 1823 enabled Giuseppe to take over his post as church organist in Roncole when he was still only twelve. In the same year, his father sent him to study at the Gymnasium in Busseto directed by Pietro Seletti.

He continued his musical studies with Provesi, the bandmaster of Busseto, and was a frequent guest in the house of Antonio Barezzi, president and lea-

ding light of the local Philharmonic Society as well as a flautist in its ranks, around whom the village's musical life revolved. With the musical guidance of Provesi and the patronage of Barezzi, the Philharmonic players had achieved a good technical standard and were often asked by neighbouring parishes to come and play for their church services and functions. It was in response to requests such as these that the young Verdi wrote four marches for the Good Friday Procession and *Le Lamentazioni di Geremia* (The Lamentations of Jeremiah), all among his earliest works.

He also became engaged to Barezzi's daughter Margherita in 1831. With the assistance of his future father-in-law and staunch supporter (who was also helping him financially), Verdi won a Monte di Pietà scholarship that enabled him to move to Milan where, at the age of 19, he tried to enrol at the Conservatory. Failing to pass the entrance examination in 1832, he continued to study privately with the opera conductor Vincenzo Lavigna, who also conducted at La Scala.

On Provesi's death, Verdi was obliged by the terms of his scholarship to return to Busseto, and he succeeded Provesi as band-master in 1836. He married Margherita in the same year and began to compose

him to write another opera, even though he was still overwhelmed by the death of his wife and children. The 1842 La Scala premiere of *Nabucco* was a complete triumph and marked the start of Verdi's domination of Italian opera that would last for the next fifty years. *"Va' pensiero"*, the famous chorus of the exiled Jews in *Nabucco*, is a supreme example of popular choral writing, and Verdi's choruses would contribute significantly to the success of many of his later operas, especially since his Italian audiences saw them as thinly-veiled expressions of the patriotism that would spark off the revolutions leading to the unification of Italy in 1848.

His fourth opera was very much the outcome of

Portrait of Margherita Barezzi. Museo Teatrale alla Scala, Milan.

Portrait of Bartolomeo Merelli. Museo Teatrale alla Scala, Milan.

the music for a first opera. *Oberto, conte di San Bonifacio* was performed for the first time at La Scala in 1839 and was so well received that the powerful impresario Merelli offered him a contract to write other operas. Verdi had already moved to Milan, but the tragic deaths first of his two children and then Margherita herself in 1840 brought him to the verge of nervous collapse. He was certainly in no frame of mind to compose the comic opera Merelli had commissioned from him, and not surprisingly, the La Scala premiere of *Un giorno di regno*, was a miserable failure. Undeterred, Merelli persuaded

evenings spent in the company of the writers and poets who frequented the literary salons of the Milanese aristocracy. The 1843 premiere of *I Lombardi alla prima crociata*, based on the poem by Tommaso Grossi, was a triumph; this, together with the earlier success of *Nabucco*, led to performances of his operas in both Paris and London, and he began to reap the rewards of international fame. It was during this period that he fell in love with Giuseppina Strepponi, who had sung the soprano role so brilliantly in the premiere of *Nabucco*.

It is difficult to assess the exact extent of Streppo-

Piazza della Scala, Milan. Print. Civica Raccolta di Stampe Bertarelli, Milan.

ni's influence on the course of Verdi's life because she played such a variety of different roles in it even before she became his second wife. She had contributed directly to his early success by politely though firmly insisting that *Oberto* should be given a performance, and with Verdi now universally known, it was difficult for observers to understand how a singer two years his junior could have won such a special place in his professional and emotional life. Born in Lodi, Giuseppina had musical gifts that secured her a place among the more important singers of her day. She never became a *primissima donna* because her desperate need of money obliged her to accept any type of contract she could get. By the age of twenty she was already having to support her family, and shortly after, the two children she bore out of wedlock. Unusually well educated for a singer of her time, she knew French and German well, and was a competent amateur pianist.

She was the first to sing Abigaille in *Nabucco*, and it is known that her voice had already begun to deteriorate by then. She would retire from the stage shortly after, but she had already given Verdi much sound artistic advice, including the suggestion that he should ask the same figure for *I Lombardi* that Bellini had asked for *Norma*. Verdi was a frequent guest in Strepponi's dressing room during the premiere performances of *Nabucco*, and he probably found in her company something of the peace of mind that he had lost after the death of his first wife Margherita and their two children.

Although they both wished it, they did not immediately start living together. Verdi was a frequent guest in the homes of the Milanese aristocracy during the period from 1842 to 1847, and Giuseppina moved to Paris where she opened a singing school that soon became one of the best known in the French capital. They met again in Paris in November 1847 when Verdi came to supervise performances of an adaptation in the "French" style of *I Lombardi*, and they would never be separated again. Although the Italian unification movement was beginning to gather momentum, Verdi remained in Paris for a good while longer, but he eventually succumbed to nostalgia for the flat landscapes of his native Emilia. With strong encouragement from his father-in-law and protector Antonio Barezzi, he bought an estate at Sant' Agata and went to live there with Giuseppina.

They lived at first in a large town house in the centre of Busseto, where the scandal of their unmarried status provoked the violent disapproval of the people of the village, but they continued to live in this way for the next ten years. When they did eventually decide to marry in 1859, the simple ceremony was performed in the utmost secrecy in a small mountain church in the Aosta Valley, far from the prying eyes and wagging tongues of fashionable society.

As has already been suggested, it may be that the irregularity of his own situation with Giuseppina provided the inspiration for perhaps his most "au-thentic" creation, *La Traviata*, the immediate stimulus for which was a stage version of Dumas' *The Lady of the Camelias* which he saw with Giuseppina in Paris in 1852. It does not seem too far-fetched to suppose that much of the human and social truth of *La Traviata* reflected the irregularity of their own social position at the time. Apart from Verdi's temporary infatuation with Teresa Stolz, who sang in the Milan premiere of *Aida*, the couple remained united until Giuseppina's death in 1897. There can be little doubt that their life together on their large estate at Sant' Agata, or on Verdi's foreign tours supervising performances of his operas (Giuseppina even went with him to St. Petersburg in 1862 for the premiere of *La Forza del Destino* there), was essentially a happy one. Suffice it to say that she was his constant inspiration, mentor, companion and adviser, and that this more than explains the strength of the bond that kept them united for so many years.

After the Venice premiere of *Ernani* (1844) and the success of other operas including *I due Foscari* (The Two Foscari), *Giovanna d'Arco* (Joan of Arc), *Alzira*, *Attila*, *Macbeth*, *I masnadieri* (The Brigands), *Il corsa-*

On the left: oil portrait of Giuseppina Strepponi. Museo Teatrale alla Scala, Milan.
On the right: the famous singer dressed for the stage. Drawing. Gesellschaft der Musikfreunde, Vienna

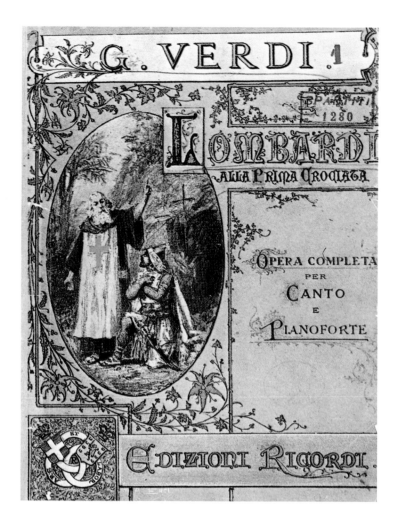

Cover of the scores of Verdi's "I Lombardi" and "Il Trovatore" in a 19th-century Ricordi edition. Archivio Storico Ricordi, Milan.

ro (The Corsair), *La battaglia di Legnano* (The Battle of Legnano), *Luisa Miller* and *Stifello*, Verdi began work on the three greatest operas – *Rigoletto*, *Il Trovatore* and *La Traviata* – that would win him universal popular acclaim.

Rigoletto, based on Victor Hugo's *Le roi s'amuse*, was first performed in 1851, and the triumphant premiere of *Il Trovatore* took place in the Teatro Apollo in Rome in 1853, by which time Verdi was already immersed in the composition *La Traviata*. The premiere at the Venice La Fenice opera house in 1853 was not a success, however. *La Traviata* was based on Dumas' *The Lady of the Camelias*, in which the life and death of a wealthy Paris courtesan are presented in movingly human terms. The subject was unconventional, then, and for the times, highly *risqué*, and to make matters worse, Verdi the innovator had given it a fully realistic treatment on stage which marked a complete break with formal eigh-

114

teenth-century opera. Gone was the sparkling effervescence of Rossini's *bel canto* writing, the aureate purity of Bellini's melodies and the warmth of Donizetti's arias. Verdi's uncompromisingly honest view of one woman's personal tragedy produced a complex musical portrait dominated by vigorous, emotionally charged rhythms and the darker psychological half-tones of subtly varied orchestration. With *La Traviata*, Verdi made opera comment directly on the real life that lay outside the theatre for the first time, and the musical and dramatic realisation of Violetta is even subtler than Dumas' portrayal of Marguérite Gautier in his celebrated novel.

Although their themes were regarded as too direct and even scandalous at the time, and public reaction was at first violently censorious, the great trilogy of *Rigoletto*, *Il Trovatore* and *La Traviata* would become perhaps the most popular of all Verdi's works.

1853 found Verdi in Paris, where preparations were under way for the first Universal Exhibition celebrating the friendship of the peoples of the world. After performances at the Paris Opéra of *Les Vespres siciliennes* (The Sicilian Vespers) in 1855, which Verdi had specially written to mark the occasion, he returned to Italy to start work on a new opera, *Simon Boccanegra*, which had its unsuccessful pre-

miere at La Fenice in Venice in 1857.

Italy was in political ferment at the time. The second war of independence broke out in 1859, and with the aid of Napoleon III of France, the Kingdom of Savoy declared war on the Austrian Empire. Verdi decided to take an active part in the political life of Italy by becoming delegate for his home town of Bussetto at the Assembly of the Provinces of Parma, which had elected to side with the House of Savoy in the conflict. In 1861 he accepted the position of Parliamentary Deputy in Turin, the capital of the Kingdom of Savoy.

His prestige as Italy's greatest national musician was enormous. In spite of his many political commitments, he began work on *La forza del destino* (The Force of Destiny, based on the Spanish Romantic masterpiece) which had been commissioned by the Russian imperial family. It was first performed at the Imperial Opera in St. Petersburg in 1862. *Don Carlos*, based on Schiller's play, was completed in his country home at Sant'Agata and triumphantly mounted at the Paris Opéra later the same year.

With Italy now a united country, Count Cavour, its first Prime Minister, asked Verdi to become a Parliamentary Deputy, with the result that his composing was seriously affected. Normally accustomed to writing two operas a year, he managed a total of

A scene from Act 1 of Verdi's "La Traviata" in the 1965 Arena production, Verona.

only seven operas during the last thirty years of his life.

He returned to opera only in 1870 after accusations that he had given in too easily to public demands. The new opera, *Aida*, had been commissioned by the Viceroy of Egypt to celebrate the official opening of the Suez Canal in 1871. The premiere was a total triumph (the universally popular opera is still considered a masterpiece) and confirmed Verdi's reputation as the greatest living opera composer. Then, after further years of silence broken only by revised versions of *Simon Boccanegra* (1881) and *Don Carlos* (1884), Verdi eventually produced *Otello* in 1887. His extraordinary *Requiem*, composed in 1874 in memory of Alessandro Manzoni, is the greatest of his non-operatic works.

Now engaged in an orderly round of musical commitments, publishing work and the running of his various estates, Verdi lived with his wife Giuseppina in their winter home in Genoa, the spa town of

Photograph of Verdi taken in St. Petersburg in 1862. Fotostudio Arborio Mella, Milan.
Below: a scene from Act 3 of Verdi's "La forza del destino". Archivio fotografico del Teatro alla Scala, Milan.

Verdi and the librettists

Verdi was usually the dominant partner in his dealings with librettists, taking an active part in the writing of the librettos he commissioned and sometimes supplying long passages of his own which his librettists then simply had to put into verse. With some (Maffei and Boito, for example) he was scrupulously tactful, but others, like his celebrated "slave" Piave, were tyrannised by him and were certainly not spared the lash of his tongue. We know very little about the Antonio Piazza who seems to have been the libret-

Aida). His librettists were certainly kept busy, and their librettos were almost commissioned as if they were episodes in some longer serial story or part-work. Verdi's relations with his translators were less incisive, and he seems to have chosen them more or less at random. Charles Nuitter (an anagram of Truinet) and Alexandre Beaume (Beaumont), both of them well-known playwrights (Nuitter was a friend of Wagner), translated the second version of Macbeth, and Achille de Lauzières, a music critic and composer, translated the first version of Don Carlos (the revised second version was the work of Angelo Zanardini who would later translate

"The Theatre Rehearsal". Caricature by Delfico. Villa Verdi, Sant'Agata.

tist of Verdi's first opera (which probably became Oberto at some later date). However, the pattern of Verdi's dominance over meekly acquiescent librettists was already well established by the time Solera wrote the libretto for Nabucco, although some of his librettists became real collaborators and even helped to mount performances when necessary (Maffei, Boito, Ghislanzoni, Giuseppe Montanelli who advised Verdi on Simon Boccanegra while exiled in Paris, Emanuele Bardare who finished the libretto of Il Trovatore after the death of Cammarano, and Camille Du Locle who wrote the libretto for Don Carlos and advised Verdi on the plot of

Wagner into Italian). It is still not known for certain who translated Les Vespres siciliennes. Arnaldo Fusinato is the traditional candidate, but Verdi scholars have recently begun to think that the unknown Ettore Caimi may in fact have been the translator. Translations apart, however, Verdi's correspondence with his various librettists would fill many volumes, and it is clear that he himself was the real author of his librettos, given that he dictated the handling of the themes, supervised the literary revision of the texts (or the stage dialogues, at the very least) and was responsible for the final versions of all his librettos.

Montecatini in Tuscany, and their summer home at Sant'Agata. He also travelled extensively both in Italy and abroad, but had given up politics after refusing re-election as a Parliamentary Deputy. He was persuaded to become a Senator in 1875, but never attended Senate meetings.

And then, at this late stage in his life, he suddenly produced a comic opera, perhaps in reply to comments he was incapable of writing comedy. *Falstaff*, with a libretto by Arrigo Boito based on Shakespeare plays featuring the famous comic hero, was first performed in 1893 and is considered one of Verdi's greatest masterpieces, a courageously uncompromising and far-sighted response to the growing popularity of Verist opera. After the death of his wife in 1897, he devoted most of his time to charitable works, including the founding of his famous Casa di Riposo (Rest Home for Musicians) in Milan, and financial assistance for a wide range of charitable institutions. His death in 1901 in Milan, where he had resettled after his wife's death, was the occasion of national mourning. He was buried next to his wife in his own Rest Home for Musicians, in the chapel which their friend, the great singer Teresa Stolz, had had specially built for them.

On the left: cover of the score of "Aida" in the 19th-century Alphonse Leduc edition.

Below: photograph of the set for "Aida" in the 1961 Verona production. Stage design by Pino Cesarini.

*On the left: cover of a special issue of "Illustrazione Italiana"
marking the premiere of Verdi's "Otello".
Civica Raccolta di Stampe Bertarelli, Milan.*

*Below: cover of a special issue of "Illustrazione Italiana" marking
the premiere of Verdi's "Falstaff".
Museo Teatrale alla Scala, Milan.*

Verdi's concept of character

To those who went to operas in the Romantic period, and for those who study them now, the appearance of Verdi's characters on the opera house stages of the world was a sudden and remarkable event. They inhabit a world far removed from the playful intrigue of earlier opera plots, in which dramatic character seems little more than a temporary role assumed merely for the duration of the opera itself. By contrast, Verdi's characters have the naturalness and force of real people; we feel we are in the presence of living personalities that have life outside the confines of the opera house. A Verdian character reasons coherently, feels deeply, loves and hates with equal passion, schemes and plots, uncovers the scheming and plotting of others, gives way to tenderness and compassion, and recognises the supernatural destiny that shapes his actions while never losing sight of the everyday world in which he lives. They seem to embody both the absolute moral certainties of the Middle Ages and the passionate enquiry and finer shades of moral and psychological purpose of Renaissance man.

Critical analysis shows that the totally convincing humanity of his characters is, in fact, a by-product of the purely musical universe (complete from overall structure right down to the most detailed expressive markings in the score) in which he locates the dramatic situations and human emotions of the story he has to tell.

Although the various stages through which a work has passed during its composition can never fully be known, given that every piece of music is different and even the composer may not really know exactly how he came to compose certain parts of it, we might say that

Costume by Rudolf Heinrich for Rigoletto in Verdi's opera.

Adelina Patti, one of the great interpreters of "La Traviata".

Verdi's point of departure was invariably the character of a particular man or woman (irrespective of their dramatic importance) in the poetry, prose or dramas on which he based his plots, and his greatest gift the intuitive grasp of the psychological realities that motivate human behaviour. Even before working with his librettist, he seems already to have explored the psychology of his characters, their reaction to events they themselves may have brought about, the joy or suffering they experience as a result, and the final meaning which both audience and characters attribute to these events.

With Verdi, all these considerations come before and in a sense conceal the musical problems which are professionally his real concern. The decisions he needs to make about the music he is about to write seem those of a playwright, not a composer. He wrote Falstaff, a work of extraordinary freshness and vitality, at the age of eighty-eight, and the music itself does not seem to have worried him overmuch. As in all his operas, the cues are marked, the voices are well combined, the orchestra is skilfully deployed to produce heightened emotional effects when necessary, and each character is given a clear musical identity (some recurrent use of a distinctive interval or harmonic progression, perhaps), but none of this is theoretical and none needs explanation, because the music itself is self-explanatory. Verdi's true genius is his natural flair for matching music to dramatic situation. Until the situation was clear in his mind, the music would not come, but it was effortless when it did. If he was unhappy with certain lines or passages of a libretto, the result was invariably less than satisfactory music.

His interest in the situations and psychologies of his characters and the mechanics of his plots was such that he declared himself unable to write music for isolated lines, no matter how well written or suggestive, if they had no intelligible dramatic context. It is important, too, that he was plain-spoken and direct with impresarios and singers right from the start of his career, avoiding the diplomatic compromises, flattery and insincerity that were, and still are, so much a part of the operatic world.

So it was not just the music that interested him, but also the exact scene of which it was to be part, and even the kind of voice best suited to playing a particular role. While supervising rehearsals for Aida with his usual care, for example, he commented that he was quite willing to do without the particularly beautiful voice of one of his singers because it was not matched by the experience needed to sustain a role as complex as that of Amneris. "You know the libretto for Aida," he remarked to Giulio Ricordi, "so you'll also know that Amneris requires an artist of great dramatic and emotional intensity who can literally command the stage. What hope is there of finding this in a singer who is virtually a debutante? A beautiful voice alone (and how difficult it is to judge beauty in an ordinary room or an empty theatre) is not enough for that part. I don't really care very much about what people call perfection in singing. True, I like to have parts sung the way I want, not the way someone else wants, but I can't actually provide the voice itself, the spirit, that certain something people usually call "being possessed" but should really be called sparkk." In addition to the kind of communicativeness required of singers in moments of high dramatic tension, an opera also has to present a whole range of dramatic moods in purely musical terms. Verdi places his skill in matching and contrasting characters, in alternating comic, tragic and violent scenes, or brilliant with slower, more reflective music, entirely at the service of the artists who perform in his operas. His music becomes a natural medium for the expression of what they have inside themselves.

The baritone Antonio Magini-Coletti in the role of Iago in Verdi's "Otello". Museo Teatrale alla Scala, Milan.

The mezzosoprano Maria Waldmann in the role of Amneris in the La Scala premiere of "Aida" in 1872. Miniature.

The baritone Victor Maurel as Falstaff. 19th-century engraving. Civica Raccolta di Stampe Bertarelli, Milan.

Stage		

32 operas

Title	Librettist	Date & place of 1st perf.
Oberto, conte di San Bonifacio	T. Solera (recte A. Piazza)	17.11.1839 La Scala, Milan
Un giorno di regno (Il finto Stanislao)	F. Romani	5.9.1840 La Scala, Milan
Nabucco	T. Solera	9.3.1842 La Scala, Milan
I Lombardi alla prima crociata (1st version)	T. Solera	11.12.1843 La Scala, Milan
Ernani	F.M. Piave	9.3.1844 La Fenice, Venice
I due Foscari	F.M. Piave	3.11.1844 Teatro Argentina, Rome
Giovanna d'Arco	T. Solera	15.2.1845 La Scala, Milan
Alzira	S. Cammarano	12.8.1945 Teatro San Carlo, Naples
Attila	T. Solera	17.3.1846 La Fenice, Venice
Macbeth (1st version)	F.M. Piave & A. Maffei	14.3.1847 Teatro La pergola, Florence
I masnadieri	A. Maffei	22.7.1847 Her Majesty's Theatre, London
Jerusalem (2nd version of I Lombardi)	A. Royer & G. Vaâz	26.11.1847 Opéra, Paris
Il corsaro	F.M. Piave	25.10.1848 Teatro Grande, Trieste
La battaglia di Legnano	S. Cammarano	27.1.1849 Teatro Argentina, Rome
Luisa Miller	S. Cammarano	8.12.1849 Teatro San Carlo, Naples
Stiffelio (1st version)	F.M. Piave	6.11.1850 Teatro Grande, Trieste
Rigoletto	F.M. Piave	11.3.1851 La Fenice, Venice
Il trovatore	S. Cammarano & L. Bardare	19.1.1853 Teatro Apollo, Rome
La traviata	F.M. Piave	6.3.1853 La Fenice, Venice
Les Vàpres siciliennes (Italian vers. Giovanna di Braganza, then Giovanna de Guzman, finally I Vespri Siciliani)	C. Duveyrier & E. Scribe	13.6.1855 Opéra, Paris
Simon Boccanegra (1st version)	F.M. Piave	12.3.1857 La Fenice, Venice
Aroldo (2nd vers. of Stiffelio)	F.M. Piave	16.8.1857 Teatro Nuovo, Rimini
Un ballo in maschera	anon., but by A. Somma	17.2.1859 Teatro Apollo, Rome
La forza del destino (1st version)	F.M. Piave	10.1.1862 Teatro Imperiale St Petersburg
Macbeth (2nd vers.)	C. Nuitter & A. Beaumont	21.4.1865 Théâtre Lyrique, Paris
Don Carlos (1st vers.)	C. Du Locle (Ital. trans. A. De Lauzières)	11.3.1867 Opéra, Paris
La forza del destino (2nd version)	A. Ghislanzoni (edited)	27.2.1869 La Scala, Milan
Aida	A. Ghislanzoni	24.12.1871 Opera House, Cairo
Simon Boccanegra (2nd version)	A. Boito (edited)	24.3.1881 La Scala, Milan
Don Carlos (2nd vers.)	-	10.1.1884 La Scala, Milan
Otello	A. Boito	5.2.1887 La Scala, Milan
Falstaff	A. Boito	9.2.1893 La Scala, Milan

Vocal		
1 mass	Requiem for 4 voices, choir & orchestra	1874
6 other sacred works	Pater noster for 5 voices and chorus	1880
	Ave Maria for soprano & strings	1880
	Four Sacred Pieces	1886-95
2 hymns	Suona la tromba	1848
	Hymn of the Nations	1862
many early works	including:	
	Domine ad adiuvandum	1830-31
	Stabat Mater	1830-31
	Io la vidi	1833
	Il V Maggio	1836?

Songs		
22 works	including:	
	Six Romances	1833
	L'esule	1839
	L'abbandonata	1849

Instrumental		
early works	including:	
	Pieces for various instruments & orchestra	1829

Chamber		
1 string quartet	Quartet in E minor	1873

Liszt

Portrait of Franz Liszt. Musée Carnavalet, Paris.

Franz Liszt, the great virtuoso pianist, conductor and composer who would revolutionise piano technique and anticipate Wagner in his orchestral compositions, was born in Raiding in 1811. He received his first musical tuition from his father, Adam Liszt, an accountant in the service of Prince Esterbéz at Eisenstadt when Haydn was conductor of the court orchestra there. He quickly saw that his son had extraordinary musical talent.

Franz gave his first concerts in Oedenburg in 1820 when he was only nine, and so impressed a group of Hungarian magnates and noblemen that they agreed to finance tuition for him in Vienna. He studied there with Czerny and Salieri and, in his first concert in 1821, stunned a discerning Viennese audience with his virtuosity. The Liszt family

123

Liszt in a drawing by Jean Auguste Dominique Ingres. Winifred Wagner Collection, Bayreuth.
On the right: portrait of Marie d'Agoult. Drawing by Théodore Chassèriau, 1841. Louvre, Paris.

left Vienna towards the end of the year and settled in Paris, where he soon established a reputation as a phenomenal pianist, shamelessly exploiting his virtuoso command of the instrument more in the manner of a circus performer than a serious concert artist. His 'performing-dog tricks', as he himself called them, astounded the aristocratic audiences of salons he performed in, and he soon became the idol of Paris, although he also gave performances in France, Great Britain and Switzerland.

However, Liszt never allowed his lucrative concert career to affect his more serious studies as a composer, which he continued in Paris under the guidance of Paër and Reicha. In 1824, Paër persuaded the Paris Opéra to commission a short melodramatic piece from the young composer. The result, *Don Sancio or The castle of love*, first performed in 1825, was soon forgotten, but Liszt refused to be discouraged and in the meantime pursued his career as a virtuoso pianist. It is no accident that his only important compositions of this period, the Studies, were specifically written to develop the unexplored technical potential of the piano which his 'performing-dog tricks' had made him aware of, even though his own technical command was absolute by the standards of the day. Published in Marseilles in 1826, the 12 Studies (originally intended to be 24) were primarily designed for his own use. The technical problems of the piano obviously

appealed to his imagination rather more than the fatuous libretto of *Don Sancio*, and produced a highly personal creative response of an entirely different order. No other pianist had ever written piano music such as this, in which technical inventiveness and imagination could at times even reach the heights of poetry. The extraordinary importance of these early Studies is borne out by the fact that they would be republished, with only slight revision, as the *Transcendental Studies*, one of the great masterpieces of piano literature.

Around the time of his father's death in 1827, Liszt decided to start teaching as a way of bringing some order to his chaotically busy life, and also began to study philosophy and the Classics enthusiastically. In 1834 he began a long affair with the Comptesse Marie de Flavigny, wife of the Compte D'Agoult, and moved with her first to Switzerland and then to Italy, composing as he went a set of short piano pieces that would later be revised to become *Anneés de pèlerinage* (Years of pilgrimage).

His concert career reached its peak in the years from 1839 to 1847: Vienna was followed by a triumphal return to Hungary, new triumphs in Prague and Germany, and then Paris again. He broke definitively with Marie de Flavigny in 1844 and began new relationships with the actress Charlotte de Hagn and the ballerina Lola Montès. In 1847 he began a long friendship with Princess

The keyboard of Liszt's piano. Wagner Gedenkstätte, Bayreuth.

The Princess Carolyne von Wittgenstein with her daughter Marie.

Pius IX in 1868, and henceforth wore an abbot's robes. From then on he divided his time between Budapest, Weimar and Rome. He was made president of the National Academy of Music in Budapest, and his oratorio *Christus* was well received in Weimar.

Liszt's last years were spent travelling and working throughout Hungary, France, Italy, Luxembourg, Great Britain and Germany. He continued to compose and was present at triumphant performances of Wagner's operas in Bayreuth. He died there only a few days after a performance of *Tristan und Isolde* on 31 July 1886, three years after Wagner himself in 1883.

The greatness of Liszt's pianism is most evident in the 24 *Studies* (1838), the 12 *Transcendental Studies* (1838) and the three sets of *Anneés de pèlerinage* (1836-77). Of his works for piano, the most notable are the Sonata in B minor (1852-53), the *Mephisto Waltz* and his late piano works in general. His greatest works for piano and orchestra are the two Concertos in E flat major and A minor, and *Totentanz* (The dance of death), a macabre fantasy on the

Caricature of Liszt on horseback by A.J. Lorentz.
Bibliothèque Nationale, Paris.

Carolyne von Sayn-Wittgenstein.
After years of composing virtually continuously, Liszt became settled in Weimar in 1848, where he had been conductor of the orchestra since 1842, a post which involved organising and directing the court's concert and opera seasons. Under his baton, the orchestra became one of the best in Europe, and his composing also benefited greatly, with the result that orchestral works became central to his output. In fact, the *Symphonic poems* were written during this period.

Meanwhile, after hearing *Rienzi* for the first time in 1844, he was working body and soul to make Wagner's music better known. Liszt considered Wagner a god of music, and their lifelong friendship was further strengthened when Wagner married Liszt's daughter Cosima. During his intensely creative period in Weimar, Liszt directed performances of all the most controversial operas of the time, including Berlioz' *Benvenuto Cellini* and *Lelio*, and Schumann's *Genoveva*, but the combination of a disastrous performance of Cornelius' *The Barber of Baghdad* and the hostile conservatism of the city ended his happy period there. He moved to Rome in 1865, where he received Minor Orders from Pope

126

Liszt conducting a performance of an Oratorio in Pest. Gesellschaft der Musikfreunde, Vienna.
Below: Silhouette of Liszt as a priest in Rome in 1870 by F. Schulze. André Meyer Collection, Paris.

Dies Irae theme.

It cannot be denied that Liszt's music is uneven and has at times serious shortcomings. What made him great was his ability to respond to and then fully assimilate the musical ideas and trends of his time. Undoubtedly, he owed much of this ability to the places and cultures he knew and lived in. Born in an area where the Viennese Classical style had reached its full maturity, and educated during his formative years in Vienna itself, he moved to Paris as an adolescent when it was virtually a show-case for all European culture, and spent the rest of his life in close contact with Italian melodrama and the great German instrumental tradition. Perhaps no other musician – of his time or any other – has ever accumulated such a wealth of experience or had so many opportunities to make good use of it.

This, together with his unusually out-going, generous character and an instinctive willingness to see and bring out the best in others, even to the detriment of his own great talent, largely explains why Liszt, although certainly not one of the greatest composers of his time, was nonetheless one of the age's most important and interesting musicians, and one of the key figures of the Romantic era in general.

Stage		

Sacred

4 masses	Missa quattuor vocum	1848
	Missa solemnis	1855
	Missa choralis	1865
	Mass for the Hungarian coronation	1867
1 requiem	Requiem for soloists, male chorus, organ and brass	1867-68
2 oratorios	Christus	1855-67
	Die Legende von der heiligen Elisabeth	1857-62
various works	including:	
	4 Pater Nosters	1846-69
	2 Ave Maria	1846-69
	2 Te Deum	1853-59
	6 Psalms	1855-81
	Cantico del sol di S. Francesco	1862
	Hymn to the Virgin Mary	1869
	Tantum ergo	1869
	Septem Sacramenta	1878
	Die heilige Cäcilia Legende	1874
	Via Crucis	1878-79
	Rosary	1879
	Pro Papa	1880c

Secular

various works	including:	
	Für Männergesang (12 pieces)	1842-59
	The Four Elements (4 pieces)	1844-48
	Weimars Volkslied (6 pieces)	1857
	Morgenlied	1859
	Gaudeamis igituur	1869
	Ungarisches Königslied	1883

Orchestral		

13 symphonic poems	Les Préludes	1848
	Ce qu'on entend sur la montagne	1848-49
	Tasso	1849
	Héroäde funèbre	1849-50
	Prometheus	1850
	Mazeppa	1851
	Festklänge	1853
	Orpheus	1853-54
	Hungaria	1854
	Hunnenschlacht	1857
	Die ideale	1857
	Hamlet	1858
	Von der Wiege bis zum Grabe	1881
2 symphonies	Fuast Symphony	1854
	Dante Symphony	1855-56
other works	including:	
	Festmarsch zur Goethe Jubiläumsfeier	1849
	Three Funeral Odes	1860-66
	Radetsky March	1865
	Hungarian March	1876

Concertos		

2 piano concertos	E flat major	1830-49
	A major	1839
other piano works	including:	
	Totentanz	1849
	Fantasia on popular Hungarian themes	1852

Chamber		

various works	including:	
	Duo for violin and piano	1832-35
	3 Elegies for various instruments	1874
	Am Grabe Richard Wagners for string quartet and harp	1883

Songs		

approx. 80 works and collections	including:	
	Three Petrarch Sonnets	1838-39
	Die Loreley	1841
	Mignons Lied	1842
	Es war ein Könog in Thule	1843
	Hohe Lieb	1849c
	Gebet	1878c
	Verlassen	1880

Piano		

various works	including:	
	Harmonies poétiques et religieuses	1834-52
	Album d'un voyageur	1835-36
	Années de pèlerinage (three years)	1836-77
	24 Studies	1838
	Transcendental Studies (after Paganini)	1838
	Hungarian Rhapsodies (various sets)	1839-85
	Transcendental Studies (12)	1851
	Sonata in B minor	1852-53
	2 Légendes	1863
arrangements and transcriptions	including:	
	Réminiscences de Norma (Belini)	1841
	Réminiscences de Don Juan (Mozart)	1841
	Rigoletto, Paraphrase de concert (Verdi)	1859
3 piano duets	including:	
	Fest polonaise	1876
2 works for two pianos	including:	
	Concerto Pathétique	

Organ		

12 works	including:	
	Prelude and Fugue on the name BACH	1855
	Requiem for Organ	1883

128

Wagner

Portrait of Richard Wagner. Margarey von Stockar Collection, Zurich.

Richard Wagner, the son of a low-ranking civil servant, was born in Leipzig in 1813. After his father's death the family moved to Dresden, where his mother remarried. Richard followed a normal course of school study until his interest in music was kindled when he heard Beethoven's Seventh and Ninth Symphonies. He began to have music lessons, but in all important respects he was always a self-taught musician.

Wagner went to study at the famous Thomasschule in Leipzig (where Bach had taught) and wrote his earliest significant compositions in the 1830s, including a piano sonata, a number of concert overtures and the Symphony in C major. These were followed in 1835 by an opera, *Das Liebesverbot oder Die Novize von Palermo* (The love ban or The novice of Palermo) which was given a single performance the same year. At the age of 23 he was appointed conductor of the Magdeburg Opera where, with tireless energy, he mounted an astonishing number of opera perfor-

The house where Wagner was born in Leipzig, in a painting by Franz Stasse. Wagner Museum, Tribschen.

Wagner's mother, Johanna Rosina Pätz, in a painting by Ludwig Geyer. Wagner Gedenkstätte, Bayreuth.
On the right: Ludwig Geyer, Wagner's stepfather. Self-portrait. Wagner Gedenkstätte, Bayreuth.

mances, making the best use he could of the modest resources at his disposal. Although his only previous experience of conducting and concert-giving had been as a chorus master in Würtzburg in 1834, Wagner proved a more than able producer of opera, and went on to become one of the century's leading conductors, as well as one of the first modern conductors in the sense we now use the term.

He married the actress Minna Planer shortly after moving to Königsberg in 1836, and two years later, the couple moved to Riga where Wagner had been appointed director of the local opera house. It was here that he began work on the libretto and music of his next opera, *Rienzi, der letzt der Tribuner* (Rienzi, the last of the tribunes).

After Riga, Wagner decided to try his fortune in Paris, completing *Rienzi* (although doubtful of the wisdom of doing so since he was extremely short of money) and immediately starting work on *Der fliegende Holländer* (The flying Dutchman). However, he was obliged by poverty to sell the French version of the libretto (*Le vaisseau fantôme*, The ghost ship) to

the Paris Opéra, which explains why even now in France and Italy the opera is still referred to by both names. *The flying Dutchman* took practically the whole of 1841 to write and represents a truly astonishing advance in Wagner's composing technique. The 1842 premiere of *Rienzi* at the Dresden Opera (to whom Wagner had sent the score) was a total triumph, one of the most successful opera performances of the entire century, but the premiere of *The flying Dutchman* a few months later at the Dresden Court Opera in 1843 was less successful, although Wagner was appointed director of the Royal Opera in Dresden the following month. From then on, the city became a prison to him, largely because of its narrow-minded provinciality, but it also became an important new source of musical experience. He persuaded the sovereign to sponsor outstanding performances of Gluck's *Armide* and *Iphigénie en Aulide*, and Beethoven's Ninth Symphony, advocated a thoroughgoing reform of the opera house's entire organisation, and invited Spontini to conduct his *La vestale* in person. He also completed *Tannhäuser*,

Panoramic view of Dresden in a 19th-century print. Wagner Gedenkstätte, Bayreuth.

Below: the Dresden Hoftheater in a print of 1841. Wagner Museum, Tribschen.

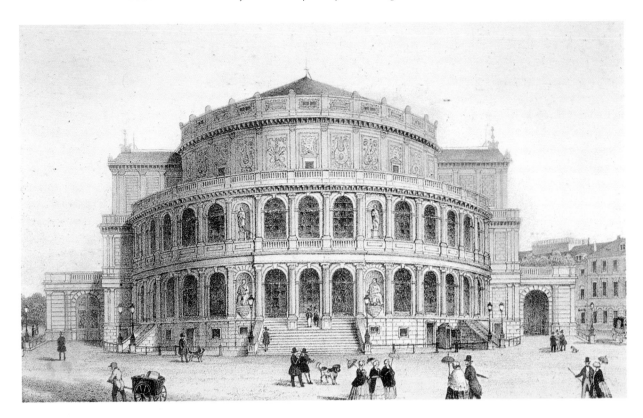

although its premiere in 1845 was not particularly successful.

Wagner's historic encounter with Liszt took place in Berlin in 1845. The famous pianist was a great admirer of Wagner's operas, and their first meeting marked the start of a long-lasting friendship. In the meantime, the political situation in Saxony, as in the rest of Germany, was slowly deteriorating, and Wagner found himself siding with the more liberal and progressive of the various factions, whom he openly supported in the abortive revolution of 1849. He was with Bakunin on the barricades in Dresden, but was forced to flee the city to avoid arrest as a terrorist. Welcomed in Weimar by Liszt, whose generosity and support further strengthened their friendship, he later moved to Zurich when his exile from Germany was made official.

Virtually the next ten years of Wagner's life were spent in Zurich, where he began publishing books and articles (including *Art and Revolution*) explaining his aesthetic theories.

Liszt courageously mounted a performance of *Lohengrin* in Weimar in 1850, the opera Wagner had composed between 1846 and 1848, describing it as a

Wagner's wife, the actress Minna Planer, in a watercolour by Clementine Stockar-Escher. Wagner Gedenkstätte, Bayreuth. Below: the Dresden court theatre during the premiere of Wagner's "Rienzi", and a poster advertising the performance of "Rienzi" in Dresden on 20 November 1842. Wagner Gedenkstätte, Bayreuth.

Villa Wesendonck on Lake Zurich in a watercolour of 1857. Heck-Rieter Collection.
On the right: programme for a concert by Wagner at the Casino in Zurich on 15 January 1850. Wagner Museum, Tribschen.

poem extolling man's remotest origins.
During his ten years of exile and extreme poverty in Zurich, Wagner also brought the planning of his visionary opera cycle *Der Ring des Nibelungen* (The ring of the Nibelungs) to an advanced stage, and continued to conduct in order to make money. He was forced to flee to Venice in 1858 owing to the scandal of his relationship with Mathilde Wesendonck, wife of the financier who had given Wagner lodgings on his estate. Alone in Venice, he began work on the score of *Tristan und Isolde* (which he completed in Switzerland in 1859). Besieged by creditors, he moved on to Paris, where his operas seemed more likely to win acceptance.
With the help of the Princess Metternich, Wagner was able to have *Tannhäuser* performed, but the protection afforded him by the French court led to hostility in Paris' more snobbish circles, which was inflamed still further by his refusal to move the ballet in *Tannhäuser* from the beginning of Act One to Act

Dienstag den 15. Januar 1850.

Viertes
Abonnements-Concert

der

allgemeinen Musikgesellschaft

im grossen Casino-Saale.

Programm.

Erste Abtheilung.

1. Ouverture aus Wilhelm Tell von Rossini.
2. Cavatina für Sopran aus Attila von Verdi, gesungen von Fräul. Josephine Morra.
3. Lore-Ley, } zwei Lieder für Bariton von Kücken, gesungen von Herrn Roth, Mitglied
   Maurisches Ständchen, } der hiesigen Oper.
4. Introduktion und Variationen für die Guitarre von Vois. vorgetragen von Fräul. J. Morra.
5. Recitativ und Aria für Sopran aus Figaro's Hochzeit von Mozart: „O, säume länger nicht," gesungen von Fräul. Corrodi.

Zweite Abtheilung.

6. Sinfonie in A dur Nr. 7 von L. van Beethoven, durch verstärktes Orchester unter Direktion des Herrn Kapellmeister Richard Wagner aus Dresden.
7. „Jamais, jamais," von Ciccarelli, } gesungen von Fräul. J. Morra.
   „Rataplan", Chanson de Madame Malibran, }
8. Adagio und Polonaise für Horn von Körnlein, vorgetragen von Hrn. Schrenk, Mitglied der Kapelle.
9. Duett für zwei Sopran aus Maria Padilla von Donizetti: „a figlia incauta", gesungen von Fräulein Corrodi und Fräul. J. Morra.

Der Anfang ist um 6 Uhr Abends.

Billets zu 1 Gulden sind beim Conciorge im Casino und Abends an der Kasse zu haben.

Aktuariat
der allgemeinen Musikgesellschaft.

Two. As a result, the opera was greeted by cat-calls and whistles from at least half the audience, and Wagner left the French capital a bitter and disappointed man. He separated from his wife and moved to Vienna, where he remained from 1862 to 1864. Worried that *Tristan und Isolde* had still not been performed (it was considered too difficult to sing), he began work on a new opera, *Die Meistersinger von Nurnberg* (The mastersingers of Nuremberg), and set off on his travels again, partly for artistic reasons, but also to avoid the creditors who were making his life increasingly unbearable. He moved from Vienna to Stockholm in 1864, where he was visited by an emissary of King Ludwig II of Bavaria with the message that the young monarch wished Wagner to join him in Munich as a musician and friend. King Ludwig generously paid off all Wagner's debts and, among other things, sponsored the first triumphant performance of *Tristan und Isolde* in Munich in 1865, when an astounded and admiring audience was literally moved to tears.

King Ludwig's over-enthusiastic interest in the composer aroused hostility in his court, and once again Wagner was forced to flee to Switzerland, leaving behind him the place where he had hoped to realise his grandiose operatic dreams. However, this was nothing compared with the scandal that broke in 1865. Wagner was sharing lodgings with one of his closest friends, the pianist and conductor Hans von Bülow, and his wife Cosima, Liszt's daughter, and Wagner's enemies were not slow in discovering and making public his real relationship with the wife of his faithful friend. The couple denied everything, naturally, and even involved King Ludwig in the ensuing war of accusation and counter-accusation in the local press. In the end, Cosima left her husband and moved with Wagner and her two children to Tribschen in Switzerland where the composer completed *The mastersingers of Nuremburg* in the security of his new family home. Again thanks to King Ludwig, the opera was performed in Munich in 1868 to great public acclaim, although the

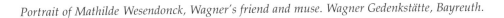

Portrait of Mathilde Wesendonck, Wagner's friend and muse. Wagner Gedenkstätte, Bayreuth.

critics seemed baffled by the music.

Wagner and Cosima were able to marry in 1870. In the same year, he composed one of his loveliest instrumental works, the *Siegfried idyll*, which was dedicated to his new wife, and completed his planning of *The ring*.

During the 1870s, Wagner began to move towards realising his lifelong dream of creating an opera house specially designed for the performance of his operas, and of *The ring* in particular, which also meant retraining singers and musicians in his new and revolutionary concept of stage performance. As both a man of the theatre and a man of letters, Wagner believed that words and music should be the work of a single mind, which is why he always wrote his own librettos so that the drama, poetry and music of his operas would be perfectly integrated. In planning his opera house at Bayreuth, he was careful to ensure that his texts, and in particular, the unusual stressing of certain words, would be clearly audible, and that spectators would always have a clear view of the stage and not be distracted from what was happening on it.

It was only natural that an artist with ideas such as these should also take a minute interest in the mounting of his operas, or what is now called 'production'. Although amazingly plain (rough-and-ready, even) from the outside, the opera house at Bayreuth in fact embodies Wagner's reasoned opposition to the idea, current in his time, that an opera should

Photograph of Ludwig II of Bavaria, Wagner's staunch patron. Wagner Archiv, Bayreuth.
Below: the Festival Theatre at Bayreuth in a watercolour by S. Schinkel, 1876. Wagner Gedenkstätte, Bayreuth.

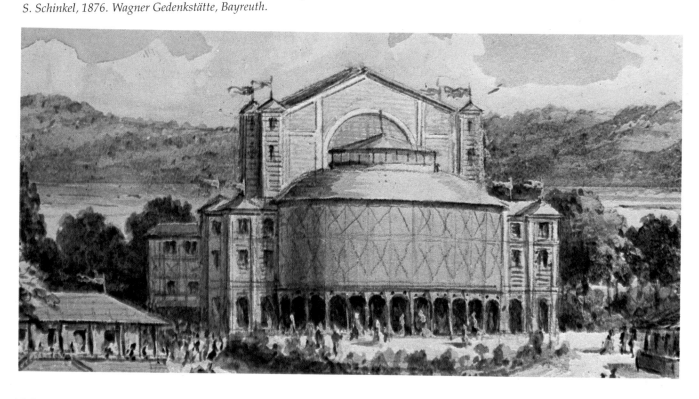

Franz Liszt with his daughter Cosima, who would later become Wagner's second wife. Wagner Museum, Tribschen. On the right: a musical meeting in Wagner's home in a painting by W. Beckmann, 1880 (from left to right: Cosima Liszt, Richard Wagner, Franz Liszt and the musicologist H. von Wolzogen). Wagner Museum, Lucerne.

simply be 'performed', and no more. His early experience in the humble opera house in Riga had convinced him that the orchestra should be positioned below the level of the stage so as to be virtually invisible, that the seating in the auditorium should be terraced to make the stage fully visible from every angle, and that the auditorium should be in darkness throughout the performance. Thus, Bayreuth does not have the boxes and sloping trapezoidal auditorium of traditional opera houses, and, a stroke of genius on Wagner's part, the orchestra is placed out of sight in a pit with the brass seated even lower so that the full splendour of their tone in loud passages never overwhelms the voices of the singers on the stage above or renders the poetry of his librettos inaudible. With the help of friends and supporters, the opera house was finally inaugurated with a complete performance of *The ring* on 13, 14, 16 and 17 August 1876.

In order to nurse his increasingly poor health, Wagner, now at the pinnacle of his fame, made frequent journeys to Italy, and in the meanwhile completed *Parsifal*, which was performed at Bayreuth in 1882. Having returned to Italy in September 1883, he died in Venice of a heart attack.

Although his early operas were inspired by Italian traditionalist opera, Wagner subsequently devoted the rest of his life to reforming the principles and practice of opera performance, and the founding of a great German operatic tradition. The early steps he took towards achieving this with *The flying Dutchman* (1843), *Tannhäuser* (1845) and *Lohengrin* (1850) culminated 20 years later in *The ring*, the epic operatic tetralogy he had begun while exiled from his native Germany. Based on the heroic legends of Nordic mythology, each of the four operas is performed on a separate day. From the musical and theatrical points of view, however, his most revolutionary opera is *Tristan und Isolde*, in which the individual arias and recitatives of traditional opera are replaced by a concept of 'continuous' melody which runs throughout the work.

Wagner made greater use of chromatic harmony than any other composer of his time, and in effect carried the principles on which tonal music is based to their logical limits. He had, therefore, a great influence on later composers such as Debussy and Schönberg.

137

Without going so far as Max Nordau, who believed that Wagner's true greatness was as a painter and that his poetry and music were merely signs of decadence and degeneration, we can certainly agree that stage design and production are at least as important as music in Wagner's revolutionary concept of the theatre. There is no need here to cite the many references to stage design and production in his theoretical writings because the detailed annotations and production notes he added to his 'libretti' from The Flying Dutchman already give us a good idea of the care he took to ensure that his stage designs would 'conspire' with his plots and music to produce an experience of total art, the Gesamkunstwerk that would remain his artistic ideal throughout his life. This said, the extent to which his rather traditional stage designs fail to match the revolutionary brilliance of his

unified concept of music and drama was well served by Quaglio's designs, which in any case established a tradition of stage design firmly based on the early Wagner productions. And yet, Quaglio's actual designs seem to offer no radical departure from the historicist pictorial taste of his age, if the inevitable Nuremberg settings of the open air scene in Act 3 and the rather irksome Gothic-type architecture of Scene 1 (complete with stained-glass windows, porticos, balconies and coats of arms) of Die Meistersinger are anything to go by. Act 2 works rather better, with less oppressive, highly pictorial settings that produce a rather attractive nocturnal ambience: Sachs' illuminated shop on the left, Eva and Walther hiding behind a hedge on the right and the ridiculous black figure of Beckmesser in the centre as he sings his serenade. The design for Act 1 of Tristan is

Angelo Quaglio's design for Lohengrin.

music still comes as something of a surprise. It is almost as if, unlike in his music, he never quite succeeded in freeing himself from the documentary, Naturalistic conventions of the age he lived in.

Wagner's stage design developed in two distinct stages, corresponding to his periods in Munich and Bayreuth, which were dominated respectively by Angelo Quaglio and Max and Gotthold Brückner. Quaglio, the descendant of a family of Italian stage designers, was active in opera (especially in Germany) during the second half of the 19th century, and worked closely with Wagner in the Hoftheater in Munich. There he designed several productions of all the pre-reform operas, and it is to him that we owe the stage design for the premieres of Tristan (1865), Die Meistersinger (1868), Rheingold (1869) and Die Walküre (1870). Quaglio's relationship with Wagner was a fertile one, and the composer must certainly have believed that his

equally famous: the enormous deck of a ship surmounted by a huge baldachin decorated with vaguely Neo-Classical heraldic and monumental designs.

The designs for the complete Ring cycle at Bayreuth are more unusual and important. With all the resources of the 'ideal' opera environment he had dreamed of finally at his disposal, Wagner made sweeping changes to the way operas were produced: a fully darkened auditorium, the orchestra concealed in a pit, 'magic lantern' projections and the use of steam to mask scene changes. But once again, his approach to the purely visual aspects of his sets was much more cautious. He contacted the painters Hans Makart and Arnold Böcklin, but nothing concrete came of it, unfortunately. We can only regret that Böcklin, the painter of The Island of the Dead in which Naturalistic conventions undergo chilling transformations, was never given the opportunity to paint sets for the shadowy world of the Ring. What followed marked Wagner's final decision to abandon any attempt at reforming the visual aspects of stage design, and as the great stage designer Adolphe Appia would later remark, his decision merely highlights the irreconcilable conflict between musical expression and scenic and gestural expression, almost as if the theatre, an eminently social art form, were unable to keep pace with the evolution of radical individual expressive modes in poetry and easel painting.

Joseph Hoffman, a moderately talented Viennese painter, adhered scrupulously to Wagner's libretto annotations in producing his series of designs for the Ring, and the result was a combination of Naturalism at its most grandiose and heroic in the sets — huge caves, boration resulted in a series of extraordinarily eclectic sets. The Grail scene, with its clear references to Siena cathedral (at Wagner's express wish) and actual written inscriptions, is imposingly monumental, an architectural creation in the true sense rather than architectural pastiche. By contrast, Joukovsky's lighter and more graceful garden scene in Act 2 is an essay in the virtually defunct Naturalism of earlier decades with elements that anticipate the Art Nouveau of the next century. After Wagner's death, and at Cosima's personal insistence, stage design at Bayreuth fossilised into total conservatism. The Brückner's, now officially entrusted with preserving the word of the hallowed master, were responsible for all subsequent revivals: Tristan in 1886, Die Meistersinger in 1888, Tannhäuser in 1891, Lohengrin in 1894 and, finally, The Flying

'Klingsor's Garden' painted by Max Brückner from a sketch by Paul von Joukovsky for Parsifal. Richard Wagner Gedenkstätte, Bayreuth.

ancient oaks, rocks, pools, etc. – and barbaric medievalism in costumes and interiors (especially in Gibicunghi's production of Götterdämmerung).

However, Hoffmann's failure to translate his pictorial ideas into functional theatre sets in the real sense soon led to a break with Wagner two years before the inauguration of the Festspielhaus. His place was take by Max and Gotthold Brückner, highly skilled theatre painters and directors of an important stage design studio in Coburg. Their designs for the Tetralogy (1876) were based by and large on Hoffmann's existing designs, and Emil Doepler was brought in to design the costumes. Max Brückner was subsequently appointed official stage designer at Bayreuth, and was responsible for the designs for Parsifal (1882), although the Russian painter Paul von Joukovsky was also asked to work with him. Stylistically, their colla-

Dutchman in 1901, which was the work of Max Brückner alone. The obstinate documentary realism of the sets is leavened, in one or two designs, by cautious attempts to include more contemporary pictorial styles, ranging from sumptuous Art Nouveau in Act 3 of Lohengrin and the beautifully illuminated spaces of the Feast of St. John in Act 3 of Die Meistersinger to the Impressionism of Tannhäuser. However, the vast majority of the Brückner sets are attempts to enshrine the dying echoes of the 'lessons' which the dead master had imparted years before, perpetuations of an 'authentic' Wagner tradition which his widow Cosima did her utmost to defend. 'The Ring', she wrote, 'was produced here in 1896, so there is nothing new to be discovered as regards its stage design and production.'

139

The tenor Joseph Aloys Tichatschek as Tannhäuser in the premiere of Wagner's opera. Wagner Gedenkstätte, Bayreuth.

One of the most discussed and perhaps disconcerting (though also fascinating) aspects of opera is Leitmotiv, roughly translatable as 'recurring theme'. Wagner did not actually invent Leitmotiv, although he carried it to new levels of subtlety and dramatic significance.

Since the very beginnings of opera, composers had seen that it might be possible to associate given musical phrases with certain characters, situations or locations. The oldest is perhaps the trumpet fanfare announcing the entrance of a warrior, a simple and effective means of suggesting his character and role. The sound itself was clear and extremely eloquent, and communicated its message instantaneously, working simultaneously on the mind and sensibility of whoever heard it.

Opera composers in the seventeenth and eighteenth centuries were well aware of this effect. Naturally, there were as many different versions as there were composers to write them, but they all used phrases more or less of the same type, simply constructed and limited in dramatic range and effect.

Thus, there were well established musical formulas not only for storms, bird-song, the murmuring of waves and the din of battle, but also, by extension, for basic emotional states (love, hate, revenge, courage etc.).

Even more interesting is the fact that this new awareness of the dramatic possibilities of music was also finding its way into instrumental music, an area from which it should, theoretically, have been excluded. If composers were having difficulty in rationalising the effects that music could produce in opera, where music was allied with words, what hope was there of doing so in instrumental music which could not rely on words to clarify its exact meaning, and so risked seeming no more than a pleasurable though ultimately in-

consequential stimulation of the senses?

Vivaldi was the first instrumental composer to incorporate this new awareness in his music, although it is difficult to define exactly how his splendid 'musical themes' work in practice. Without actually imitating natural sounds, he succeeds with irresistible charm in conveying what nature is like. He communicates not concepts but images which are no less vivid for being exclusively musical.

We should not be deceived by the programmatic titles of many of Vivaldi's concertos; except in a few cases, they derive not from an attempt to imitate nature but from Vivaldi's purely musical symbolism, which seemed to need attaching to something – in Vivaldi's case, nature – after it had been composed.

In this sense, we could say that it was now realised that instrumental music (and so all music) was a completely independent art form, with the result that operatic musical themes and symbols could now cease to be merely descriptive and naturalistic (and so always external to human personality) and become musical transcodings of ideas or states of mind seen from the inside. This is exactly what Wagner did when (as Thomas Mann said) he made music, more than ever before, a means of allusion, intellectual enquiry and psychological reference.

Perhaps the most revolutionary aspect of Wagner's music is his use

P. Gamba's costume for Mime in the 1910 La Scala production of "Siegfried". Ente Autonomo Teatro alla Scala.

Two 1876 lithographs by Emil Doepler of "The Ride of the Walküre". Wagner Gedenkstätte, Bayreuth.

of all the musical and intellectual resources of the symphony in extending the emotional and dramatic range of opera and establishing new relationships between orchestra and the stage. The use of Leitmotive was crucial to his new concept of opera. They are virtually the scaffolding of the whole structure, points of reference which render the purely musical discourse of his operas orderly and immediately comprehensible to audiences.

It is the orchestra that clarifies, directly or indirectly, the actions on stage, and which in many cases carries the real burden of the opera's complex meaning. Characters express their thoughts in words, but we often perceive their more intimate feelings through the medium of the orchestra, which amplifies and sometimes even contradicts the characters' words.

In this way, Wagner succeeded in representing a vast range of ideas and things in purely musical terms: characters and the ideas associated with them, places in or aspects of nature, emotions and states of mind, and many other direct or indirect aspects of the action on stage.

His greatness is most apparent in the inventiveness of his Leitmotive, which are almost always of a disconcerting immediacy. Their non-verbal communication is instantaneous even if we do not know exactly what they represent; they take us immediately to the heart of the action. For example, when, in Rheingold, Wotan, king of the gods, comes on stage for the first time at the beginning of Act Two, his words are accompanied by the solemn chording of his Leitmotiv, so that whenever it is heard later in the opera we associate it immediately with Wotan and his home in Valhalla. Similarly, when in Walküre Brunhilde announces to Sieglinde, 'O woman, thou nurturest in the shelter of thy womb the most noble hero of the world,' the accompanying fanfare of Siegfried's Leitmotiv already introduces us to Siegfried, the hero of The ring, *before he actually appears on stage later in the cycle.*

The soprano Lili Lehmann, a famous Wagner singer. Theatermuseum, Munich.

There are many other examples, but to finish by relating Wagner's achievement in the historical development of the Leitmotiv, it need only be said that he succeeded in uniting with opera the ideas that were revolutionising music as the symphony began to assert itself in the eighteenth century.

141

Stage		

14 operas

Title	Librettist	Date & place of 1st perf.
Die Hochzeit (unfinished)	R. Wagner	composed 1832
Die Feen (The Fates)		composed 1833-34
		29.6.1888
		Court Theatre, Munich
The Novice of Palermo	R. Wagner	29.3.1836
		Magdeburg
Rienzi	R. Wagner	Court Theatre, Dresden
The Flying Dutchman	R. Wagner	21.1.1843
		Court Theatre, Dresden
Tannhäuser (1st version)	R. Wagner	19.10.1845
		Court Theatre, Dresden
Lohengrin	R. Wagner	28.8.1850
		Grossherzogliches
		Hoftheater, Weimar
Tannhäuser (2nd version)	R. Wagner	13.3.1861
		Opéra, Paris
Tristan and Isolde	R. Wagner	10.6.1865
		Königliches Hof-und
		Nationaltheater, Munich
The Master-Singers of	R. Wagner	21.6.1868
Nuremberg		Königliches Hof-und
		Nationaltheater, Munich
The Ring of the Nibelungs	R. Wagner	13-17.8.1876
(The Walkyrie, Siegfried,		Festspielhaus, Bayreuth
The Twilight of the Gods)		
Parsifal	R. Wagner	26.7.1882
		Festspielhaus, Bayreuth

Incidental music		
overtures and other works	including:	
	7 pieces for Faust (Goethe)	1832
	Overture for Faust (Goethe)	1840

Piano		
15 works	including:	
	2 Sonatas	1829
	Albumblatt	1861

Vocal		
choral works	including:	
	Gesang zur Enthüllung des Denkmais Sr.	
	Majestät des hockselingen	
	Königs-Friedrich August des Gerechten	1843
	Fünf Gedichte für eine Flauenstimme	
	(Wesendonk-Lieder)	1858
	Kinderkathechismus	1874
approx. 20 songs with piano	including:	
	Les deux grénadiers	1840
	Trois mélodies	1840

Orchestral		
10 works	including:	
	Symphony in C major	1832
	Siegfried Idyll for small orchestra	1870
	Kaisermarsch for large orchestra	1871
	Grosser Festmarsch	1876

Brahms

Photograph of Johannes Brahms. National Museum, Prague.

German instrumental music passed through four major stages of development. The first, typified by the music of Bach's sons in the mid eighteenth century, ended with the symphonic schools that grew up in both Mannheim and other less important cities. Next came Haydn and Mozart, whose works, although seemingly new and entirely without precedent, were in fact the result of a brilliant assimilation and synthesis of new musical trends and ideas not only current in Germany at the time but also imported from France and Italy. Vienna, then extraordinarily receptive to the popular art and culture of the East, provided the ideal musical environment for them to work in.

Hamburg: the Speckstrasse, the street in which Brahms was born. Museum für Hamburgische Geschichte, Hamburg.

Portrait of the young Brahms by Bonaventure Laurens. Museum für Hamburgische Geschichte, Hamburg.

Almost as a bridge linking this earlier 'Classical' period to the Romanticism of the following century, there stands the figure of Beethoven, whose assimilation of his predecessors' achievements was so personal that its true importance was understood only decades later.

Next came the Romantic phase, extending from the ardent dreams of Schubert to the tortured longings of Schumann, and culminating in Mendelssohn's somewhat restricted, though nonetheless influential, synthesis of Classical and Romantic styles. With this parabolic return to the Classicism of an earlier era, German instrumental music might well have ended with Liszt and Wagner. Liszt's fiery, revolutionary temperament had led him to attempt a fusion of music with poetry, in which sheer brilliance and suggestiveness of effect had come before purity of sound and cleanness of line – an attractive though dangerous undertaking. Wagner, on the other hand, had transferred Beethoven's massive

symphonic achievement to the stage in his epic operas.

The older instrumental forms were evidently worn out since Liszt and Wagner, the age's two most forward-looking composers, felt able to ignore them completely. It is no accident that Wagner concentrated on opera (his instrumental output is insignificant by comparison) while Liszt wrote no chamber music or symphonies (in Classical terms, his two concertos for piano and orchestra are concertos only in name).

And then, as if by some strange paradox, a new musical sensibility emerged. The great German instrumental works had had little to say to Liszt and Wagner, who had wanted to do away with traditional forms entirely, but the next generation of composers, seemingly indifferent to the revolutionary fervour of their famous predecessors, adopted a completely different approach to the older Classical genres. They accepted the past as given, seeing it as a musical reality that could be made to live again once it had been fully assimilated and understood. Johannes Brahms was one such composer.

It was through the advocacy of Schumann, by then a respected composer of unquestioned distinction, that Brahms first attracted the notice of the German musical public. Schumann's famous article 'New Ways', the last piece he wrote for *Neue Zeitschrift für Musik*, a music periodical of the time, proved both a leave-taking and a prophecy, for in it he named the unknown Brahms, still a mere 20 years of age, as the composer who would carry forward the great German Romantic tradition.

Schumann's prophecy was well grounded. He had already brought the greatness of Chopin to the attention of the public, and in Brahms he saw all the signs of potential genius, the kind of versatility that could move effortlessly from choral grandiloquence to the hushed intimacy of small-scale melody. Behind a certain fieriness of temperament, Schumann had glimpsed in the young composer not only the serene poise of the true artist but also an essential modesty, two aspects of Brahms's personality that

in later life would lead him to live a life apart in a world of solitary dreams.

Brahms came from a family of modest means. His mother, Johanna, the real head of the household, was 17 years older than her husband Johann Jacob, a competent all-round musician who played the French horn and double bass, and her interest and ability in educating her children and running the home was far greater than her husband's. Johannes was deeply attached to his parents, but after lying dormant for years, the tensions produced by their profound differences in age and character eventually caused them to separate late in life, in spite of all Johannes' efforts to prevent it.

His father, although immature and temperamentally unsuited to the responsibilities of bringing up a family, was quick to note his son's musical talent, and by 1840 Johannes was already receiving tuition from Otto Cossel, before moving on Edmund Merxen, to whom he remained attached for the rest of his life.

In addition to the piano, Brahms also studied foreign languages and, most important of all, became

The young Brahms and the violinist Ede Reményi in a daguerrotype of 1853.

On the right: title-page of Brahms' "Variations" on a theme by Schumann. Biblioteca del Conservatorio G. Verdi, Milan.

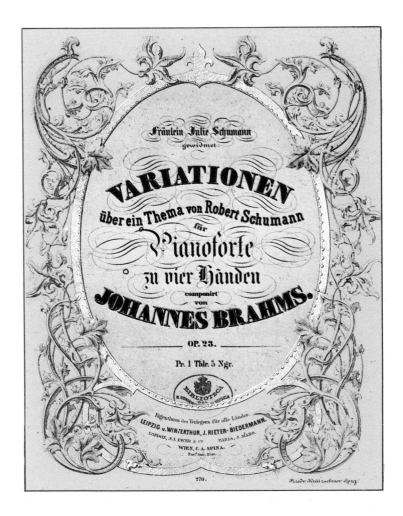

Title-page of Brahms' "Hungarian Dances" for piano duet. Wallraf-Richartz Museum, Cologne.

On the right: Robert and Clara Schumann in 1850. Print from a daguerrotype. Gesellschaft der Musikfreunde, Vienna.

an avid reader of poetry. Apart from equipping him to select the texts for his marvellous *Lieder*, his love of poetry in later life developed into a constant search for inner truth that made him avoid all forms of superficial display or attention-seeking.

The Brahms family was not well off, so Johannes accepted paid work as a piano player in a dockside tavern when he was only 13 years old.

In 1850, a Hungarian violinist named Eduard Reményi, exiled from his country after the revolutions of 1848 and 1849, came to Hamburg and happened to meet the 17-year-old Brahms. They soon became friends, and gave a series of recitals together in and around Hamburg.

Reményi's childhood friend Joachim, a celebrated concert violinist of profound musical sensibility and insight, was also quick to note Brahms's talent. The differences between Brahms and Reményi were obvious to him when he first saw them together. Reményi's out-going, worldly character, with more than a touch of snobbery and boastfulness, was less than congenial to him, but he was immediately attracted to Brahms, whose painful sincerity and social ineptness made him ill at ease in company and quite incapable of sharing a witty conversation about Liszt, Schumann and Chopin, all of whom he revered.

Brahms's meeting with Joachim was a major turning point in his life. It gave him the courage to break off his friendship with Reményi, who was now openly envious of his talent, but more important, it gave him an introduction to the musical court of Weimar, where Liszt reigned supreme, and opened the doors of Schumann's home to him.

Brahms's first meeting with Liszt in Weimar was not a success, and their mutual incomprehension kept them forever hostile and apart, but the immediate friendship he established with the Schumanns grew into a lifelong attachment, the sort of disinterested friendship and intellectual accord which Goethe described as 'elective affinity'. Each of the three found something of themselves in the others, as well as new and interesting things to learn. Brahms's shyness disappeared as if by magic in the warmth and security of the Schumann home, alive with music and filled with books, plants and the voices of children.

In 1857, he accepted the post of chorusmaster in the small Westphalian court of Detmold, whose customs and etiquette were still very much those of the previous century. Although more than presentable, Brahms was often socially careless and so quite unsuited to the rigid manners of the court, but in the end he was much more influenced by the life there than might at first have seemed possible. It was at Detmold that he made his first rapturous acquaintance with Germany's true heritage, the awe-inspiring figures who had made German culture what it was in the ages of Bach, Handel and even earlier. Moreover, the fact that he was, like the musicians of former times, a court employee rather than an independent artist like Schumann, Liszt or Wagner, produced in him a strictly practical, craftsmanlike view of his art, free of the Romantic notion that music should be the powerful expression of intensely personal feelings. His two Serenades, Op. 11 and 16, and the String Sextet, Op. 18, were the first results of this 'return to the past'.

Brahms resettled in Hamburg a year later, hoping to be made director of the Singakademie there, but his friend Julius Stockhausen was appointed instead. Disappointed, he moved to Vienna in 1862 and was appointed director of its Singakademie, but he held the post for barely a year. Having calculated that he could make a modest living from publishing his compositions and from other occasional work, he gave up all external commitments in 1864 to become a freelance musician.

Serious family problems occasionally forced him to return to Hamburg, however, and when his father and mother separated he was faced with the task of maintaining them both in separate establishments, a crippling financial burden he was to bear until his mother's death in February 1865. Typically, he refused to speak of his grief, but he received a deeply felt letter from Clara Schumann, who had continued to write to him. This letter marked the start

Vienna: a lithograph of the Opernring taken from a watercolour by Franz Alt. Historisches Museum der Stadt Wien, Vienna.

not only of a regular correspondence that was to last for the rest of their lives, but also of Brahms's secret love for Clara.

Contrary to the usual Romantic notion that life and art are inseparable, very little of Brahms's life found its way into his music. We find nothing of his emotional life, of his ambiguous relationship with Clara Schumann, for example, or his engagement to the singer Agathe von Siebold (broken off just before they were to be married) and still less of his bizarre proposal of marriage to Clara Schumann's daughter Giulia, which Clara herself indignantly rejected. On the one hand we have his life, amply documented, full of anecdote and open to investigation in every detail (although frankly incomprehensible at times), and on the other, we have his music. And yet, there seems to be no connection whatever between the two.

Brahms became a mature artist in Vienna, where his already abundant chamber works were eventually supplemented by large-scale symphonic works. A symphony he had been planning since 1854 proved so difficult to complete that in the end he reworked some of its material into his First Piano Concerto, Op. 15, completed in 1859. This intro-

Brahms conducting. Silhouette by W. Bithorn. Gesellschaft der Musikfreunde, Vienna.
Below: Brahms at the piano in a lithograph by Willy von Beckerath. Museum für Hamburgische Geschichte, Hamburg.

A photograph of Brahms in the study of his Viennese home. Photograph by Maria Fellinger, 1897. Gesellschaft der Musikfreunde, Vienna.

spective, intensely felt work, totally devoid of empty virtuosity, did not win the approval of the critics, and for years after Brahms was deterred from attempting anything on a similar scale. When, much later, he did return to the symphony, he was able to solve his earlier technical and formal problems with no difficulty whatever. The *German requiem*, Op. 45, one of his most characteristic works, was composed between 1857 and 1868 in memory of his mother. The title itself suggests the non-liturgical nature of the work, which Brahms based on his own free adaptations of Biblical texts.

The imposing solemnity of his First Symphony, Op. 68, completed in 1876, is particularly evident in its Beethoven-like first movement. The Second Symphony, Op. 73, completed the following year, seems pastoral and idyllic by comparison. Although on a smaller scale, the distinctive Third Symphony, Op. 90, completed in 1883, has more passionate themes and, like the Second, an especially fine third movement, a deeply felt though smoothly flowing *poco allegretto* with the structural clarity and melodic charm of Mendelssohn's finest *Songs without words*. Completed in 1885, the Fourth Symphony, Op. 98

has a remarkably weighty fourth movement which is in fact a *chaconne*, an ancient form of theme and variations with a repeated or 'ground' bass line, another example of Brahms's indebtedness to the past and the effortlessness with which he was able to assimilate its forms and procedures in his own work.

His other concertos are no less important: the monumental Second Piano Concerto, Op. 83, the *Double Concerto*, Op. 102, for violin and cello and, above all, the magnificent Violin Concerto, Op. 77 (1878), in which he allows himself the rare indulgence of virtuoso solo writing, only to transform it with miraculous skill into the purest lyricism.

Brahms abandoned the orchestra in later years to concentrate on chamber music, which he had continued to write throughout his life. Of special note are his numerous *Lieder*, the Violin Sonata, Op. 78, the Piano Trio, Op. 101 (1886) and the works of late 1891, the Clarinet Trio, Op. 114 and the Clarinet Quintet, Op. 115. Brahms passed his last peaceful years surrounded by a group of faithful friends, but the long and difficult journey he had to make in 1896 to attend Clara Schumann's funeral weakened his proverbially iron constitution. Cancer of the liver was diagnosed, and he wrote his last works, the desolate *Four last songs*, Op. 121 for bass and piano, based on Biblical texts, and a set of wonderful *Choral préludes* for organ, Op. 122.

Brahms died peacefully on 3 April 1897 and was buried next to Beethoven in the Währing cemetery in Vienna.

Orchestral		
4 symphonies	Symphony No. 1 in C minor	1876
	Symphony No. 2 in D major	1877
	Symphony No. 3 in F major	1883
	Symphony No. 4 in E minor	1885
2 serenades	Serenade in D major	1857-58
	Serenade in A major	1859
2 overtures	Academic Festival Overture	1880
	Tragic Overture	1880
other works	Variations on a theme of Haydn	1873
	Three Hungarian Dances	1874

Instrumental		
4 concertos	Piano concerto No. 1 in D minor	1854-59
	Piano concerto No. 2 in B flat major	1881?
	Violin concerto in D major	1878
	Double concerto in A major (violin & cello)	1887

Choral		
accompanied	including:	
	Ave Maria	1858
	German Requiem	1857-68
	Rinaldo (cantata)	1863-68
	Alto Rhapsody	1869
	Song of Destiny	1868-71
	Triumphal Song	1870-71
	Nanie	1880-81
	Gesang de Parzen	1882
solo	including:	
	Marienlieder	1859?
	5 songs for male chorus	1861-62
	26 sopular German Songs	1864?
	7 songs	1874
	6 songs and romances	1883-84
	5 songs	1888
20 canons	including:	
	13 canons for female chorus	
approx. 60 vocal quartets with piano	including:	
	3 quartets	1859-63
	Liebeslieder waltzes	1868-69
	3 quartets	1872-74
	15 new Liebeslieder waltzes	1874
	4 quartets	1874-84
	6 quartets	1888-91
approx. 20 vocal duets with piano	including:	
	4 duets 1860-62c	
	4 duets	1874
	5 duets	1875

Chamber		
strings	2 sextets	1859-65
	3 quintets	1864-91
	6 quartets	1861-75
	5 trios	1853-57
7 instrumental sonatas with piano	3 violin Sonatas	1879-88
	3 cello Sonatas	1862-86
	2 clarinet Sonatas	1894
also	Trio for clarinet, violin and piano	1891
	Clarinet quintet	1891

Organ		
15 works	Two preludes and fugues	1856-57
	Fugue in A flat minor	1857c
	Choral Prelude and Fugue on 'O Traurigkeit'	1857c
	Eleven Choral Preludes	1896

Piano		
3 sonatas	F sharp minor	1852
	C major	1852-53
	F minor	1853
6 sets of variations	including	
	16 Variations on a theme of Schumann	1854
	11 Variations on an original Theme	1856
	25 Variations on a theme by Handel	1861
	28 Variations on a theme by Paganini	1862-63
other collections	including:	
	Four Ballades	1854
	Eight Klavierstücke	1878c
	Two Rhapsodies	1879
	Fantasien (3 caprices and 4 intermezzos)	1891-92
	Three Intermezzos	1892
	Six Klavierstücke	1893
piano duet	10 Variations on a theme by Schumann	1861
	16 Waltzes	1865
	21 Hungarian Dances	1858-69

Songs		
approx. 300 songs	including:	
	Moonlit Night	1854?
	8 songs and romances	1858
	14 popular songs for children	1858
	15 romances from 'Magelone'	1861-68
	8 Lieder and songs	1871
	9 songs	1877
	7 songs	1884
	4 Serious Songs	1896

Tchaikovsky

Photograph of Tchaikovsky. Glinka Museum, Moscow.

Unlike most Russian musicians of his time, Tchaikovsky was not born into the rural or urban aristocracy of his day. His father, Ilya Petrovich, was a government mining engineer in the small town of Votsinsk, where Peter, the second of six children, was born on 7 May 1840. His mother, Alexandra Andreyevna Assier, came from a family of French immigrants. As was the custom in all well-off Russian families, Peter was given his first piano lessons at a very early age. His father moved to St Petersburg in 1850, and Peter was enrolled at the School of Jurisprudence there. Later in the same year he became a clerk (grade one) at the Ministry of Justice.

Charming, elegant and refined, Tchaikovsky went to all the best St Petersburg salons and spoke with easy confidence about the theatre and literature. His job (not a particularly demanding one) was no more than a financial necessity to him, and music was neither his favourite nor his only pastime. However, the attacks of depression that had started when he was 14 after the sudden death of his mother during a cholera epidemic, were becoming increasingly frequent. Encouraged by relatives and friends, Tchaikovsky began to want to further his knowledge of music, which had become a great comfort to him. In the autumn of 1861, he took theory lessons with one of St Petersburg's strictest and most traditional music teachers, Nikolai Za-remba, who was the first to realise the full extent of Tchaikovsky's talent and to encourage him to study seriously (even if he had to struggle to overcome the natural apathy of his pupil). "Supposing I do have talent, it's most unlikely that I'd ever be able to study now. I've become a civil servant, and a pretty bad one at that. I'm doing all I can to improve, but how can I also study basso continuo at

Photograph of the Tchaikovsky family in 1848. Peter is the first from the left. Tchaikovsky State Museum, Klin.

A view of 19th-century Moscow in a painting by Eduard Gärtner. Charlottenburg Castle, Berlin.

the same time?" Once these doubts had been overcome, however, Tchaikovsky proved anything but a lazy pupil. In 1862 he enrolled at the new St Petersburg Conservatory where he continued his harmony and counterpoint lessons with Zaremba and studied composition and orchestration with Anton Rubinstein, who persuaded him to leave his civil service job and found him pupils for private lessons that could go some way towards easing the financial problems brought on by the poor health of his father. Tchaikovsky's joy at leaving his job is evident in the euphoric tone of a letter to his sister: "One thing I am certain of: I'll become a

good musician, and I'll earn my daily bread ... When I've completed my studies, I dream of staying with you for a whole year so that I can compose a really great work in the peace and quiet of your home. Then ... off around the world!"

He completed his studies at the Conservatory in 1865. His graduation piece, the cantata *To joy* for soloists, chorus and orchestra based on the famous Schiller ode, won him a silver medal and much praise. Other compositions of this period are of only slight interest, however. Early in 1866, Anton Rubinstein's brother Nikolai offered Tchaikovsky a post as lecturer in harmony in the new Conserva-

posing, benefiting greatly from Nikolai Rubinstein's expert advice.

An Overture in F major was written in 1866 and performed in Moscow on 16 March of the same year, as well as a Festival Overture in D major, Op. 15 (perhaps the best work of this period) based on the Danish national anthem, and the Symphony No. 1 (*Winter daydreams*) in G minor.

Tchaikovsky's earliest references to specifically Russian music came in his first opera, *The Voyevoda*, begun in 1867 with a libretto by Ostrovsky. It

Anton Rubinstein in a portrait by Iljà Repin. Museum of Russian Literature, Moscow.

tory he had just founded in Moscow. Tchaikovsky accepted and moved to the ancient Russian capital, thus beginning his life as a professional musician.

"I'm gradually getting used to Moscow, but loneliness makes me sad and depressed. My theory lessons are so successful that my fears have now vanished, and I'm beginning to look more and more like a real teacher ... I'm living in Rubinstein's house. He's a kind and understanding person, quite unlike his disagreeable brother. He has given me a room next to his bedroom. When he goes to bed at night, I'm always afraid of disturbing him with the scratching of my pen since only a flimsy wall separates us."

Tchaikovsky continued to work hard at his com-

had its premiere at the Bolshoi in Moscow on 11 February 1869. A short stay in St Petersburg in the spring of 1868 brought him into contact with the group of Russian composers known as 'The Five' (Balakiref, Mussorgsky, Rimsky-Korsakof, Borodin and Cui), although he in no way shared the ideological or spiritual inspiration of the Russian nationalist movement. Although he lived most of his life in Moscow, the heart of old Russia, Tchaikovsky never saw any real need for a truly national school of composition. The combination of his extensive studies at the St Petersburg Conservatory (a bastion of 'Western' music in Russia), his

Photograph of the singer Désirée Artôt with her dedication to Tchaikovsky.
On the right: Tchaikovsky and his wife Antonina Ivanovna in a photograph of 1877. Speiser, Basle.

partly non-Russian origins, and the importance of his Swiss childhood governess Fanny Durbach channelled his creative energy into Neo-Romanticism and adherence to the principle of 'Art for Art's sake'. In Tchaikovsky's music as Giulio Confalonieri says: "We are aware of a constant presence, a 'feminine' melancholy, a langour that embraces both intellectual spleen and a vague kind of world-weariness. This langour and melancholy are in themselves both a driving force behind his works, and an aesthetic and human truth they seek to convey, in effect what attracted him to Russian songs and popular dances as a source not of nationalistic reinstatement but of wistful melancholy, the regret of knowing one can never play a certain game, the image of some good that has been denied, lost from the very start through the operation of a personal destiny of alienation, exclusion or renunciation."

The first real affair of his life with the Belgian singer Désirée Artôt in 1868 proved an unhappy one. The symphonic poem Fate, Op. 77 of the same year was followed in 1869 by the more important overture *Romeo and Juliet* which is still the most performed of all his works.

Although Tchaikovsky's next opera, *The Oprichnik* (1870-72), has a typically Russian subject, set in the period of Ivan the Terrible, it alternates Russian dances and themes with distinctly Italian sets and situations. However, he made much more original use of national elements in the Symphony No. 2 *Little Russian* in C minor, Op. 17, inspired by Ukrainian folklore. The Quartet in D major, Op. 11, of 1871 was strongly influenced by The Five, and is his best chamber work.

Tchaikovsky was never at peace, however. The more rewarding his composing life seemed, both professionally and financially, the more unbearable his life as a teacher at the Conservatory became. However, the music he composed in this period does not contain the strongly autobiographical elements so important in his later works. On the contrary, his desire often seems to have been to impress his public with brilliant, virtuoso composition, a decision that resulted in such pieces as the Symphony No. 3 *Polish* in D major, Op. 29 (1875), the fantasy-overture *Francesca da Rimini*, Op. 32 (1876), the ballet *Swan Lake*, Op. 20 (1875-76), and the Piano Concerto No. 1 in B flat minor, Op. 23 (1874-75).

Scene from the 1865-66 La Scala production of "Swan Lake". Ente Autonomo Teatro alla Scala, Milan.
Below: the ballerina M. Pliseckaya as Odette in "Swan Lake". Glinka Museum, Moscow.
On the right: poster advertising the Moscow premiere of "Swan Lake" in 1877.

Through the intercession of one of his pupils who attended Nadezhda von Meck's musical evenings, the aristocratic patroness began to take an interest in Tchaikovsky and listened to some of his music. She wrote to him enthusiastically in 1876, offering him work. Thus began one of the strangest musical and platonic friendships in all history. Although they remained extraordinarily close for some 13 years, the couple never actually met and never even heard each other's voices, although they lived

brother Anatole. The marriage was formally dissolved with divorce proceedings.

Tchaikovsky's music changed appreciably from this moment on. The moral and spiritual collapse of 1877 was to be permanently reflected in his music, to the extent that every note of it was charged with his mental and physical suffering. This is particularly evident in the Symphony No. 4 in F minor of 1877, dedicated to Nadezhda von Meck. Tchaikovsky spent some time in Italy on his travels abroad, and finished his extraordinarily melodic opera *Eugène Onegin* there. It was given its premiere at the Malyj Theatre in Moscow on 29

Madame von Meck and her young daughter Liudmilla.
Photograph. Biblioteca del Conservatorio G. Verdi, Milan.
Below left: title-page of Tchaikovsky's 4th Symphony. Museo Civico Musicale, Bologna.
On the right: title-page of Tchaikovsky's "The Queen of Spades".
Conservatoire Library, Paris.

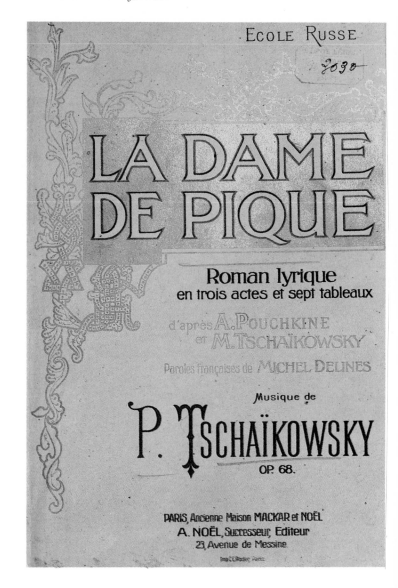

in the same city. The composer's marriage to Antonina Milyukova in 1877, a total disaster that lasted barely a few days, ended with his return to his sister on her estate at Kamenka. The experience shook his already unstable personality to its foundations and brought him to the verge of complete mental collapse. His doctors were so alarmed that they recommended a complete change of life, and he left Moscow and Russia in October with his

March 1879. He was composing very quickly now that Nadezhda von Meck had guaranteed him a generous income of 6,000 roubles a year, which enabled him to leave the dreaded Conservatory and lead a comfortably extravagant life in Moscow, alternating with journeys to France and Italy. Tchaikovsky's life now becomes little more than the story of his music and his professional successes. In the 15 years of life left to him, he composed two further piano concertos in G major, Op. 44 (1879-80) and E flat, Op. 75 (1893), the brilliant Violin Concerto in D major, Op. 35 (1878) and the String Trio in A minor, Op. 50, dedicated to the memory of Nikolai Rubinstein.

Perhaps his best opera, *The Queen of Spades*, in which his favourite theme of Fate is dramatically

A. Benois' stage design for "The Queen of Spades". Benois-Tcherkessoff Collection, Paris.

underlined by vigorous repeated melodies, was composed in 1890. However, his best work of the period was written for orchestra: a group of four suites (the last one, *Mozartiana*, is a transcription), the *Capriccio Italien*, Op. 45 (1880), the monumental *'1812' Overture*, Op. 49 (1880), the symphonic poem *Manfred*, Op. 58 (1885) and the Symphony No. 5 in E minor, Op. 64 (1888). The famous ballet *The sleeping beauty* of 1890 was followed by another ballet, the *Nutcracker*, Op. 71, in 1891-92, a charming, lightweight piece like his two previous ballets, *Swan lake* and *The sleeping beauty*. However, while the languid sentimentality of the two earlier ballets often ran the risk of mawkishness, the new ballet entirely avoids the danger with a subject that allows Tchaikovsky to display his powers of musical characterisation (often verging on the grotesque) at their most brilliant and assured. His music for the ballet shows an amazing range of instrumental invention and orchestration which

157

A scene from Tchaikovsky's "The Sleeping Beauty".
Ente Autonomo Teatro alla Scala, Milan.
Below: title-page of the Jurgenson (Moscow) edition of
Tchaikovsky's ballet "The Sleeping Beauty".
Wagner Museum, Lucerne.

reaches its peak in the moving *Waltz of the flowers*.
The theme of Fate returns once again in the Symphony No. 6 *Pathétique* of 1893, his greatest and most ambitious orchestral piece. In a letter to his nephew Vladimir Davidov ('Bob') dated February 1893 when he was still composing the symphony, Tchaikovsky says:

"I wish I could describe the pleasant mood the writing of this new work has put me in. You will recall that in the autumn I destroyed the best part of a completed symphony I had already orchestrated. I was right to do so because it was pretty worthless stuff, an empty display of notes with no real inspiration at all. Well, during my trip to Paris I had the idea for a new symphony based on a programme that I wish no one to know about, a programme so well concealed that no one will be able to discover it even if they rack their brains to the utmost. As it unwinds, this programme gradually conveys my most intimate feelings. While sketching the symphony in my head on my journey, I burst into tears more than once, as if seized by total desperation. On returning, I started writing and worked so hard that I had finished the first movement in less than four days, and the others were already perfectly clear in my mind. The form of this symphony is unusual in many ways. For example, the finale is to be a slow *adagio*, not a noisy *allegro*. You can have no idea how happy I am to know that I'm not finished yet, that I can still create."

Tchaikovsky conducted the premiere of the *Pathétique* in St Petersburg on 28 October 1893 while a cholera epidemic was raging in the city. A few days later, while dining with friends in a restaurant, he drank (perhaps intentionally) a glass of unboiled water from the River Neva. He died in agony on 6 November.

D. Louradour's stage design for Tchaikovsky's ballet "Nutcracker". Bibliothèque de l'Opéra, Paris.

Stage		
12 operas (3 unfinished)	including: The Voyevoda 1867-68	
	Eugene Onegin	1879
	The Maid of Orléans	1881
	Mazeppa	1884
	The Queen of Spades	1890
	Iolanthe	1892
3 ballets	Swan Lake	1877
	The Sleeping Beauty	1890
	The Nutcracker	1892
10 suites of incidental music	including: The Snow Maiden (Ostrovsky)	1873
	Hamlet (Shakespeare)	1891

Choral		
5 sacred works	Liturgy of St John Chrysostom	1878
	Nine Liturgical Choruses for chamber choir	1885
22 secular works	including: Ode to Joy (Schiller)	1865
	The Evening	1881

Piano		
approx. 30 works	including: Sonata in C sharp minor	1865
	Scheros à la russe and Impromptu	1867
	Romance in F minor	1868
	Sonata G major	1878
	Dumka	1886

Chamber		
4 string quartets	B minor (no number)	1862-64
	No. 1 in D major	1871
	No. 2 in F major	1874
	No. 3 in E flat major	1876
1 string sextet	Souvenir de Florence	1889-90
1 string trio	Trio in A minor	1881-82

Symphonies		
6 symphonies	No. 1 in G minor ('Winter Daydreams')	1866
	No. 2 in C minor ('Little Russian')	1872
	No. 3 in D major ('Polish')	1875
	No. 4 in F minor	1877
	No. 5 in E minor	1888
	No. 6 in B minor ('Pathétique')	1893
6 overtures	including: The Tempest	1864
	1812 Overture	1880
3 fantasy-overtures	Romeo and Juliet	1869
	Francesca da Rimini	1876
	Hamlet	1888
2 symphonic poems	Fate	1868
	Manfred	1885
2 serenades	for small orchestra	1872
	for strings	1880
4 suites	No. 1 in D minor	1878-79
	No. 2 in C major	1883
	No. 3 in G major	1884
	No. 4 ('Mozartiana')	1887
also	Capriccio Italien	1880

Instrumental		
3 piano concertos	No. 1 in B flat minor	1874-75
	No. 2 in G major	1879-80
	No. 3 in E flat major	1893
1 violin concerto	D major	1878

Songs		
approx. 100 works	including: 10 sets of 6 romances	1869-93
	1 set of 7 romances	1880
	1 set of 12 romances	1886
	1 set of 16 romances	1883
	6 duets	1880
	Love and Nature	1870
	Musical Joke	1892

Mahler

Portrait of Gustav Mahler. Albertina Graphische Sammlung, Vienna.

Gustav Mahler was born on 7 July 1860 in Kaliste, a small Bohemian town on the border with Moravia. He began piano lessons in 1866 with Viktorin, chorus master at the opera house in Jihlava, the important Moravian city in which the Mahler family had settled.

He continued studying the piano with Brosch, and made such rapid progress that he gave his first public piano recital in 1870. After spending the following year in Prague where he attended the Neustäder Gymnasium, he returned to Jihlava to continue his studies at the Gymnasium there. Concerned as ever about his son's education, his father took him to Vienna in 1875 and succeeded in obtai-

ning an audition with Julius Epstein, Professor of Piano at the Vienna Conservatory.

On Epstein's recommendation (he later became Gustav's piano teacher), his father enrolled him at the Conservatory, where he graduated brilliantly in 1878. During his stay in Vienna he made money by giving piano lessons and, in the summer of 1880, became conductor of the orchestra at Bad Hall, a small spa town, where he gave performances of operettas and musical farces.

Virtually nothing remains of the music Mahler planned or actually wrote during this early period. Much of it was lost or deliberately suppressed by Mahler himself. All that survives of any importance is *Das klagende Lied* (The song of lament), a cantata for soloists, chorus and orchestra which he began in 1878 and finished in 1880. Its failure to win the Beethoven Prize was a bitter disappointment to him, and he was obliged to seek other work. Thus began his 'calvary', his dual existence as a composer in his own right and an interpreter of other composers' works, which was to become a source of continual anguish to a man as restless and obsessive as he was.

The Bad Hall theatre, Vienna. Österreichische Nationalbibliothek, Vienna.
On the right: Gustav Mahler on the podium. Silhouette by O. Böhler. Österreichische Nationalbibliothek, Vienna.
Below: title-page of Mahler's 1st Symphony in D major. Österreichische Nationalbibliothek, Vienna.

162

He was appointed director of the Landestheater at Ljubljana for the 1881-82 season, and after again spending the summer in Vienna, moved to Olomouc in Moravia as director of the Stadttheater. His brilliance as a conductor first became evident there in performances of Flotow's *Martha* and Bizet's *Carmen*.

In 1883 he was appointed deputy director of the Court Opera in Kassel, where the director Wilhelm Treiber left him free to mount performances of Meyerbeer's comic operas.

Working conditions were far from ideal in Kassel, however, and Mahler resigned in 1885, moving on to conduct at the summer festival in Münden, where he gave much-acclaimed performances of Beethoven's Ninth Symphony and Mendelssohn's oratorio *Paulus*. During his months at Kassel, Mahler wrote his first five *Lieder* for voice and piano, the *Lieder und Gesänge aus der Jugendzeit* (Songs of youth) and produced an unorchestrated version of his first important song-cycle, *Lieder eines Fahrenden Gesellen* (Songs of a wayfarer).

He was appointed director of the Prague Deutsches Landestheater for the 1885-86 season, conducting works by Gluck, Mozart, Beethoven and Wagner, and in 1886 became deputy director of the Leipzig Neue Stadttheater, a post he subsequently resigned from. Unexpectedly finding himself without work, Mahler was helped by the musicologist Guido Adler, who succeeded in having him appointed director of the Royal Opera in Budapest, where he mounted brilliant performances of Wagner's *Das Rheingold* and *Die Walküre*, and Mozart's *Don Giovanni*.

His success as a composer did not, however, match his fame as a conductor. The premiere of his First Symphony in Budapest, which he himself conducted, was a total fiasco. To make matters worse, his father, mother and a sister all died within the space of a year, and he was faced with the task of suppor-

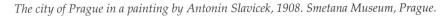

The city of Prague in a painting by Antonin Slavicek, 1908. Smetana Museum, Prague.

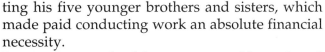
Two photographs of Alma Mahler, the composer's wife.
Below: title-page of the score of "Das Lied von der Erde" which
Mahler composed in 1907-08. Österreichische Nationalbibliothek,
Vienna.

ting his five younger brothers and sisters, which
made paid conducting work an absolute financial
necessity.

By 1890 his own health was poor, and he resigned
from his post at the Royal Theatre after a disagree-
ment with its new intendant. Thanks to the support
of Brahms and the great Hamburg music critic
Hans von Bülow (a sincere admirer of his genius as
a conductor), he succeeded in being appointed the
first director of Hamburg's Stadttheater, where
among other works he directed performances of
Italian opera (Verdi's *Falstaff* and Puccini's *Manon
Lescaut*) and also a performance of Tchaikovsky's
Eugene Onegin. His discovery during this period of
Des Knaben Wunderhorn (The magic horn of youth),
a collection of medieval legends and tragic, grotesque or simply painful poetic reminiscences of the
Thirty Years' War published between 1888 and
1899, proved a decisive event in his composing life,
and resulted in one of his greatest song-cycles.

In the meantime, he was making progress with his
Second Symphony in C minor (1887-94), one of his
most complex and ambitious works. The Third
Symphony in D minor, in many ways a spiritual
continuation of the Second and possibly the lon-

164

gest symphony ever written, was composed between 1893 and 1896. The splendid Fourth Symphony in G major, completed in 1900, marks the end of this first major phase in Mahler's composing life. Its genesis was extremely complex, and it has been regarded as rather 'small-scale', but it is a uniquely serene (though also at times ironic) work of real Mozartian clarity with delicate orchestral shading and wonderful *cantabile* melodies at times reminiscent of Schubert.

In 1892, Hans von Bülow, now ill, offered Mahler the directorship of Hamburg's subscription concerts, a post which effectively made the 30-year-old conductor the arbiter of Hamburg's musical life for the next five years, and so also a key figure in carrying forward the Viennese musical tradition. He resigned from his post at the Hamburg Stadt-theater in 1897 but, thanks to his international fame as a conductor he was soon appointed Kapellmeister and artistic director of the Vienna Opera House, a post he was to hold for the next ten years.

The move to Vienna started a new phase in Mahler's creative life. The Fifth Symphony in C sharp minor, an important stage in the clarification of his idiom, was followed by the Sixth in A minor (1903-5), and the Seventh in E minor (1904-5), his most ambitious middle-period work. The Sixth, although based on his experience of nature, is of a final desolation that seems to anticipate the hallucinatory, unreal sounds of Berg and Schönberg's early Expressionist compositions, while in the Seventh the yearning to be at one with nature becomes a grotesque, even trivial self-parody. Composed in the summers of 1906 and 1907, the monumental Eighth Symphony in E flat major is scored for soloists, organ and an enormous chorus and orchestra, and is in fact called the *Symphony of a Thousand*.

Mahler's marriage to Alma Schindler (1902), the birth and death of his first child Maria Anna (1902-7) and the termination of his association with the musical life of Vienna (riven by vituperative artistic and professional jealousies) in 1907 are the key biographical events that influenced his final creative years.

The most important works of this period are *Das Lied von der Erde* (The song of the earth, 1907-8), a song-cycle based on German translations of ancient Chinese poetical texts, and the Ninth Symphony in D major (1909-10). Mahler spent the summers of his last years in a house at Toblach and in the United States, where he conducted concerts with the New York Philharmonic Orchestra and

Fifth Avenue, New York, in a painting by Colin Campbell, 1907. Historical Society, New York.

operas at the Metropolitan. He began work on a Tenth Symphony in 1910 (which he never finished) and conducted his last concert in New York in 1911. Exhausted and extremely ill, he returned to Vienna, where he died on 18 May 1911.

An enigmatic figure both as a man and as an artist, an exceptionally gifted conductor, and universally acclaimed as one of the nineteenth century's most important musicians, Mahler's genius as a composer was never fully recognised. Even until long after his death, his works were considered the incidental achievements of a man whose true vocation was the interpretation of the music of other composers. His constant efforts to bring reorganisation and reform to opera performance, and his pioneering insistence on the conductor's total control over not only the orchestra but also every other aspect of opera performance (production, lighting, sets, costumes) were welcomed and applauded throughout his life. His works have enjoyed a considerable revival since the Second World War, and he is now seen as both the composer who carried the German symphonic tradition to its logical limits, and the forerunner of Arnold Schönberg's revolutionary break with the entire Western tradition of tonal music.

Symphonies		
10 symphonies	Symphony No. 1 in D major ('Titan')	1884-88
(1 unfinished);	* Symphony No. 2 in C minor ('Resurrection')	1887-94
symphonies with	* Symphony No. 3 in D minor	1893-96
* have chorus	* Symphony No. 4 in G major	1899-1900
or solo singers	Symphony No. 5 in C sharp minor	1901-02
	Symphony No. 6 in A minor	1903-05
	Symphony No. 7 in E minor	1904-05
	* Symphony No. 8 in E flat major	
	('Symphony of a Thousand')	1906-07
	Symphony No. 9 in D major	1909-10
	Symphony No. 10 in F sharp major (unfinished)	1910
also	Nordische Symphonie (lost)	1882?

Vocal		
42 works for voice	Lieder und Gesänge aus der Jugendzeit	1880-83
& orchestra or	Lieder eines fahrenden Gesellen	1883-85
voice & piano	Lieder aus 'Des Knaben Wunderhorn'	1888-89c
	Kindertotenlieder	1901-04
	Sieben lezte Lieder (Rückert Songs)	1901-04
also	Das klagende Lied (cantata)	1878
	Das Lied von der Erde (The Song of the Earth)	1907-08

Debussy

Portrait of Claude Debussy painted by Jacques-Emile Blanche in 1902. Jobert Collection, Paris.

The Debussys, an ancient family of Burgundy stock, had been farmers since 1600. The musician Claude-Achille was born in Saint Germain-en-Laye in 1862, where his parents had a small china shop at the time. He was educated by his paternal aunt Clémentine in Paris, where she was involved with the art collector Achille-Antoine Arosa, Claude's godfather.

Relatively little is known about Debussy's childhood, but his first experience of music came during a visit to the Riviera, where he received piano tuition from Giovanni Cerutti, an Italian teacher. Having won a state scholarship, he enrolled at the Paris Conservatory in 1872 where Marmontel, his piano teacher, quickly recognised his exceptional musical talent. He also studied harmony with Emile Durand and, briefly, the organ with César Franck, supplementing his grant by giving private piano lessons and accompanying wealthy amateurs. This periodic employment in rich families often took him far away from Paris, and his journeys to Italy and Russia were to have a particularly profound effect on his emotional and intellectual life. His employment as a pianist in the household of Marguérite Wilson-Pelouze led to a culturally stimulating sojourn in her magnificent castle at Chenonceaux in the company of other artists and writers such as George Sand.

In 1880, at the age of eighteen, Debussy entered the service of Nadia von Meck, Tchaikovsky's famous patroness, and travelled with her around Europe (he was able to see Wagner's *Tristan und Isolde* in Vienna). Impatient of the traditional harmony he was being taught at the Conservatory, he had already begun setting texts by De Musset to music and had written the recently rediscovered Piano Trio in G.

He also spent three summers (1880-82) with Nadia von Meck, playing for the family and teaching music to her many children, who remembered Debussy as 'a cheerful though subtle Frenchman who never stood still for a moment and brought much-needed life to the stuffy atmosphere of our home'. However, it was the journey to Russia that proved most crucial to his artistic development because he discovered the music of Mussorgsky, who had just died in the military hospital in St Petersburg. Mussorgsky's splendidly formless structures and spontaneously naïve pictorial imagery had a profound effect on Debussy's development as a composer. He was also much impressed by the gypsy and country folk music he heard there. His real cultural life in Paris began late in 1881 when he met the family of the architect Vasnier, an extremely open-minded intellectual whose wife, a fine singer, was to be the first to sing many of his early songs.

Debussy's musical and intellectual stance was coloured by the two most important artistic movements of his day, Symbolism in literature and Impressionism in painting, which had rejected anything formal, academic or merely passive. Not surprisingly, the reaction of official taste had been scornful. On his return from Rome, where he had lived from 1885 to 1887 in the Villa Medici after winning the Prix de Rome with his cantata *L'enfant prodigue* (1884), Debussy became increasingly identified with the artistic innovation of his time. In Rome, he had produced two orchestral works, *Zuleima*, and *Le printemps* (Spring) inspired by Botticelli's famous painting, both of which were strongly criticised for their anti-conformism by the examining board of the Académie, which later failed to see the originality of his third obligatory composition as Prix de Rome prize-winner, *La demoiselle élue* (The blessed damozel, 1886-87), based on texts by Dante Gabriel Rossetti.

Debussy became familiar with the music of Wag-

ner in the six years from 1887 to 1893, and although he disapproved of it in public, many critics have felt that this was a pose adopted to conceal his admiration and fear of the German composer's music. Though he considered Wagner 'an old poisoner', the influence of his music is certainly apparent in *La demoiselle*, *Pelléas et Mélisande* and *The martyrdom of St Sebastian*.

Back in Paris in 1888, Debussy broke off his long relationship with Gaby Dupont to marry Lily Texier, and continued his friendships with the Symbolists, all of whom were firm supporters of Wagner. In particular, he went to the Tuesday soirees at the house of the poet Stéphane Mallarmé, and it was his verse which inspired Debussy's first great mas-

Nijinsky in "Prélude à l'après-midi d'un faune", for which Debussy wrote the music. Drawing by Léon Bakst from "Comoedia ilustrée", 15 May 1912. Bibliothèque de l'Opéra, Paris.

LES BALLETS
DE MONTE-CARLO

terpiece, *Prélude à l'après-midi d'une faune* (Prelude to the afternoon of a faun, 1894). Mallarmé's poem is a vision of women seen in a summer afternoon's torrid heat, and Debussy's music is a masterly rendering of the erotically charged, hallucinatory atmosphere of the poem. It was successful with the audience at its premiere in 1894, but the critics were baffled. Mallarmé, however, was enthusiastic, and wrote to Debussy: 'Your rendering is in complete accord with my text, except that it goes even further, penetrating still more deeply to the heart of its nostalgia and the rich, deeply felt ambiguity of its light'. *L'après-midi* is typical of Debussy's subtle, suggestive music: a feeling of incompleteness, of total vagueness, with wisps of themes that never seem to be fully developed.

Having gone on to compose first the *Trois chansons de Bilitis* (1897) for voice and piano, and then the three Nocturnes (1897-98) for female chorus and orchestra, Debussy concentrated on music for the piano, producing his famous *Suite Bergamasque* (1895-99). His only opera, *Pelléas et Mélisande*, based on the play by Maurice Maeterlinck he had seen in Paris in 1893, was also begun in this period. Its premiere ten years later at the Opéra Comique in Paris on 30 April 1902 produced a mixed response of bitter controversy and wild enthusiasm, and ended Debussy's friendship with Maeterlinck, who had publicly attacked Debussy's refusal to allow a certain singer, a friend of Maeterlinck's, to sing in it. It seems that Maeterlinck did not hear the opera until 1920, when Debussy was already dead. Shortly after the performance, he wrote to Mary Garden: 'I had vowed to myself that I would never go to see

Léon Bakst's stage design for Debussy's "Prélude à l'après-midi d'un faune". Musée d'Art Moderne, Paris.

Mary Garden as Mélisande in Debussy's "Pelléas et Mélisande". Inghelbrecht Collection, Paris.
On the right: one of Léon Bakst's costumes for "Martyre de Saint Sebastien", with text by Gabriele D'Annunzio and music by
Claude Debussy.

Pelléas et Mélisande, but yesterday I broke faith with myself, and I'm a happy man. Thanks to you, I have understood my own work for the first time.' In *Pelléas et Mélisande*, Debussy created a new, elusive idiom in which melody is often based on triadic motifs. According to one critic (Lockspeiser), 'the greatest achievement of Debussy's mature years was the transformation of opera into poetry'.

Pelléas was immediately followed by a piano piece, *Les estampes*, and Debussy began work in 1903 on his greatest masterpiece, *La mer*, three symphonic sketches for orchestra. Debussy wrote to the composer André Messager in 1903: 'You perhaps don't know that I was always destined for the wonderful life of the sailor, and that only the vicissitudes of life have prevented me from following my true voca-

tion'. The theme of water, one of Debussy's favourite symbols, is found in many of his works, including *Pelléas*, where it becomes a crucial musical and narrative *Leitmotif*. The whole opera is filled with its brooding presence: the fountain, the stormy sea, the well, and glittering surfaces at times crystalline, at others opaque and impenetrable. Debussy was obsessed by the changing nature of water – by turns still or agitated, clear or opaque – seeing in its depths the powerful and even tortured presence of unconscious feelings and thoughts.

After *La mer*, Debussy began work on his second set of *Images* for piano, published the *Suite bergamasque* and *Iberia* in 1905, and completed a little piano suite, *Children's corner*, dedicated to Chouchou, his daughter by his second marriage, in 1908, to Emma

170

Moyse Bardac, a woman of high social rank. He realised the following year that he was seriously ill with cancer and began to take morphine to make the pain more bearable, but he continued to work and compose, even when he was so ill that he could not leave his bed. The first book of *Préludes* for piano was completed in 1910, and in the meantime Debussy was able to meet the most important European composers of his day. He met Richard Strauss, Germany's leading contemporary composer, in Paris in 1906 and subsequently wrote an article about him (later published in *Monsieur Croche antidilettante*, a collection of his music criticism), and, in 1910, Gustav Mahler, whose music was ridiculed in Paris (it was considered too Schubertian and Slavic).

There was much controversy over the differences between French and German music during this period, and the nationalistic rather than purely musical nature of the debate was a foretaste of the conflict that would overwhelm Europe shortly after. These were the years of the Triple Alliance between Germany, Austro-Hungary and Italy, and the Triple Accord between France, Russia and Great Britain, and all sides were hastily arming for war. In this atmosphere of strained international relations, both Debussy and Fauré refused to take part in the French Festival in Munich.

Debussy met Igor Stravinsky in 1910. They often held widely differing musical views, and their friendship was not a particularly smooth one, but they did, in fact, admire each other's work enormously.

In February 1911 he began work on incidental music for *Le martyre de Saint Sebastien* (The martyrdom of St Sebastian), Gabriele d'Annunzio's five-act mystery play which was performed on 22 May 1911 at the Théâtre du Châtelet in Paris with choreography by Fokine and costumes by Leon Bakst. It was not a success, however, in spite of Debussy's wonderfully evocative music. Between 1910 and 1915 he completed his *Préludes* and *Etudes*, universally regarded as masterpieces of twentieth-century piano music, which were followed in 1912 by the ballet *Jeux* (Games), composed for Diaghilef's Ballet Russe from an idea suggested by Nijinsky, the dancer and choreographer. Another ballet for children, *La boite à joujou* (The toy box) followed in 1913. His last work, the Violin Sonata, was composed in 1917. He died in Paris in 1918. Although he composed sporadically and unevenly, Debussy succeeded above all in rendering the

An illustration from the score of Debussy's "Boite a joujoux" (The Toy-Box) published by Durand in Paris in 1913.
Biblioteca del Conservatorio G. Verdi, Milan.

fleeting, intangible aspects of human consciousness in music. He founded no school and offered no theoretical formulation of his idiom based on experimentation with timbre and harmony and the musical expression of our awareness of nature.

Stage		
7 operas	including:	
	Pelléas et Mélisande (lyric drama by Mauruce Maeterlinck)	1902
	The Martyrdom of St. Sebastian (Mystery by Gabriele D'Annunzio)	1911
ballets	including:	
	Jeux (Poème de danse)	1913
	The Toy Box (children's ballet)	1913

Orchestral		
10 works	including:	
	Le Printemps (symphonic suite)	1886-87
	Fantasia for piano and orchestra	1889-90
	Prélude à l'après-midi d'une faune	1892-94
	Nocturnes (Nuages, Fâtes, Sirènes)	1898-99
	La mer (three symphonic sketches)	1903-05
	Two Dances for harp and orch.	1904
	Images	1908-12

Choral		
8 works	including:	
	L'enfant prodigue (cantata)	1884
	Zuleima (symphonic ode	1885
	La Damoiselle élue	1887
	Trois chansons de Charles d'Orléans	1908
	Ode à la France	1916-17

Songs		
46 works and/or sets	including:	
	Paysage sentimental	1883
	Cinq poèmes de Baudelaire	1887-89
	Ariettes oubliées	1888
	Trois mélodies de Verlaine	1891
	Fâtes galantes (1st set, 3 songs)	1892
	Proses lyriques (4 songs)	1892-93
	Chansons de Bilitis (3 songs)	1897
	Fâtes galantes (2nd set, 3 songs)	1904
	Trois ballades de François Villon	1910
	Trois poèmes de Stéphane Mallarmé	1913

Chamber		
10 works	Piano Trio	1880
	String Quartet	1893
	Chansons de Bilitis (2 flutes, 2 harps & celeste)	1900
	Rhapsody for saxophone & piano	1903-05
	First Rhapsody for clarinet	1909-11
	Petite pièce (sight-reading piece for clarinet competition)	1910
	Syrinx for solo flute	1912
	Cello Sonata	1915
	Sonata for flute, violin and harp	1915
	Violin Sonata	1917

Piano		
23 works and/or collections	Gypsy Dance	1880
	Two Arabesques	1888
	Râverie	1890
	Ballade (or Slavic Ballade)	1890
	Dance (or Styrian Tarantelle)	1890
	Romantic Waltz	1890
	Nocturne	1890
	Suite bergamasque (4 pieces)	1890-95
	Mazurka	1891
	For the Piano (suite of 3 pieces)	1901
	Estampes (3 pieces)	1903
	From a Sketch Book	1903
	Masks	1904
	The Happy Isle	1904
	Images (1st set, 3 pieces)	1905
	Images (2nd set, 6 pieces)	1907
	Children's Corner (6 pieces)	1906-08
	Homage to Haydn	1909
	La plus che lent (waltz)	1910
	12 Preludes (Book 1)	1910
	12 Preludes (Book 2)	1913
	Berceuse heroïque	1914
	12 Studies (Book 1 and Book 2)	1915
works for piano	Little Suite (4 pieces)	1889
	Scottish March on a popular theme	1891
	Six Ancient Epigraphs	1914
works for 2 pianos duet	Lindaraja (habanera)	1901
	En blanc et noir (3 caprices)	1914

Stravinsky

Portrait of Igor Stravinsky painted by Jacques-Emile Blanche. Musée des Beaux-Arts, Rouen.

Igor Fyodorovich Stravinsky was born in the small summer resort of Oranienbaum on the Gulf of Finland in 1882.

The second son of Fyodor Ignat'yevich Stravinsky, a well known bass in the St Petersburg Imperial Opera, Igor began to play the piano at an early age and was soon able to improvise on it. Indeed, he shocked his family with his open dislike of systematic study, whether of harmony or the piano itself. So close was his early identification with the instrument that in later life he was unable to compose without the aid of a piano.

Considering him 'eccentric', Stravinsky's parents made him study law at university, but in the meantime he listened to a lot of music, especially Tchaikovsky, Glinka and Rimsky-Korsakof, whom he met at Heidelberg in 1902. In fact, it was Rimsky who induced him to start composing (a sonatina, an allegro, *Faune et bergère* (Faun and shepherdess), and in 1905 a full-scale symphony). Having composed *Feu d'artifice* (Fireworks) in 1908 to mark the marriage of Rimsky's daughter, he went on to produce *Four studies* for piano and, after the death of Rimsky, a *Chant funèbre* (Funeral song).

Stravinsky's fateful meeting with Serge Diaghilef in the following year marked the start not only of his meteoric rise to fame as a composer, but also of a friendship that, with its ups and downs, was to last for the next 30 years. Diaghilef was the first to sense the genius of the young musician, who had now acquired both a university degree and a wife but still had little clear idea of where his future as a composer might lie. He commissioned Stravinsky to orchestrate *Les sylphides*, a ballet based on Chopin piano pieces, which Diaghilef's Ballet Russe performed for the first time in the 1909 Paris sea-

feu) at the Paris Opéra in 1910 also enabled Stravinsky to meet the last of the Parisian **belle époque** writers and composers such as Marcel Proust, Maurice Ravel, Manuel de Falla and, especially, Claude Debussy, with whom he began a lifelong friendship.

His second ballet for Diaghilef, *Petrushka* (1911), was equally successful, although it had none of the oriental colouring of **The firebird.** Instead, Stravinsky made full use of the pungent rhythms of

Portrait of Serge Diaghilef painted by Léon Bakst in 1906. Russian Museum, Leningrad.

Programme of the 1910 season of the Ballet Russe at the Opéra in Paris. Bibliothèque de l'Opéra, Paris.

son. 'I had just returned from holiday,' wrote Stravinsky, 'and was settling down again to the composition of **Rossignol**, when a telegram arrived that completely changed all my plans. Diaghilef was asking me to write the music for **The firebird**'. The successful premiere of **The firebird** (*L'oiseau de*

Russian popular music. 'As I composed the music,' he recalled, 'I had a clear vision of a puppet, suddenly cut loose from its strings, which exasperates the orchestra with its diabolical cascades of arpeggios. The orchestra, in turn, replies with menacing fanfares. A terrible brawl ensues which, at its height,

Léon Bakst's stage design for Stravinsky's "Firebird". Bibliothèque de l'Opéra, Paris.

finally ends with the poor puppet lamentably and painfully collapsing on the ground.' In the Paris premiere of the ballet, the incomparable Nijinsky danced Petrushka, Tamara Karsavina the Ballerina and Enrico Cecchetti the Puppet-Master.

1913 was the year which saw the huge scandal of the Paris premiere of Stravinsky's next ballet, *The Rite of Spring* (*Le sacre du printemps*), which he wrote for Diaghilef's Ballet Russe in 1912. Its relentless rhythms, use of dissonance and revolutionary orchestration (with wind and brass predominating over strings) caused open revolt in the Paris

175

1911 stage design for Stravinsky's "Petrushka".
Wadsworth Atheneum, Hartford.

On the left: Stravinsky with Nijinsky, famous for his interpretation of the role of the puppet in "Petrushka".
Bibliothèque de l'Opéra, Paris.

audience, who until then had been used to soothing, tuneful music. Thus began the triumphant career of a piece that was to have a powerful influence on contemporary composers.

At the outbreak of the First World War in 1914, Stravinsky left Russia for good and moved to Switzerland. The Ballet Russe company was disbanded and, again at the urging of Diaghilef, Stravinsky composed **The wedding** (*Les noces*) which was not performed until 1923 in Paris. Stravinsky recalls that he worked on it in the mountains, 'in a sort of box-room piled with empty Suchard chocolate boxes ... with a fur coat around my shoulders, a leather beret on my head, my feet inside a pair of snow boots and a shawl on my knees'. **The wedding** has the unusual scoring of four pianos and percussion. Two chamberworks followed. *Renard*, produced in collaboration with the Swiss writer Charles-Ferdinand Ramuz, was commissioned by Princess Edmonde de Polignac for a small orchestra of

around 20 players. The principal instrument, the **cimbalom** (dulcimer), is usually played by Hungarian gypsies. The other piece, *Histoire du soldat* (The soldier's story), was first performed in 1917 with the financial aid of Werner Reinhardt. Stravinsky was poor (the Russian Revolution had deprived him of his income) and ill at the time, and the shoe string economics of the production forced him to compose for a handful of instruments only. 'The *Histoire* resembles the jazz band in that each instrumental category is represented by both treble and bass components.' The principal instrument is the violin, which symbolises the innocent soldier who sells his soul to the devil in exchange for a talisman that makes him rich, though unhappy. This chamber masterpiece also was composed with the aid of Charles-Ferdinand Ramuz, who derived his text from an ancient Russian fable.

Once again, it was Diaghilef who inspired the com-

On the left: Stravinsky and Picasso in a caricature by Jean Cocteau taken from the collection of Cocteau drawings published in 1923 by Stock, Paris.

Below: a scene from the 1962 production of Stravinsky's ballet "The Rite of Spring" with choreography by Nicolai Roerich.

Pablo Picasso's stage design for the premiere of
"Pulcinella" at the Opéra, Paris,
on 15 May 1920.

Below: a 1963 drawing by Cocteau for
Stravinsky's "L'histoire du soldat".

position of another major work, *Pulcinella* (1919),
based on the music of Pergolese. In the ballet,
mounted in 1920 with decor by Picasso and choreography by Massine, Stravinsky adapted eighteenth-
century musical forms to his own highly rhythmi-
cal idiom. The result marks the start of his neo-
classic period which ran completely counter to the
dodecaphonic music of the second Viennese school
which was dominant at the time. Stravinsky
composed *Mavra*, an **opera buffa**, in 1922, the
oratorio *Oedipus Rex* in 1927, the ballet *Apollon
Musagète* (with choreography by Georges Balan-
chine) in 1928, and the Concerto for piano and
orchestra in 1929. He also continued his career as a
conductor, which had started in 1923 with his
Octet for wind instruments.

After the deaths of his daughter, wife and mother,
he fled to the United States in 1939 suffering from
tuberculosis. He spent 1940 convalescing and settled in Hollywood, whose climate is similar to that
of the French Riviera.

Stravinsky's major project of the years 1947-48 was
the composition of a lyric opera, *The rake's progress*,
closely based on the native verse forms of the
English language. The libretto was written by the
great English poet W.H. Auden, who had been
recommended to Stravinsky by Aldous Huxley.
The Rake portrays the picaresque adventures of a

Stravinsky liked to conduct his own works himself.
Igor Stravinsky conducting.
Drawings.

On the right: the conductor photographed while conducting in London in 1958.

179

young man who inherits a large fortune and proceeds to lose both it and his soul with the assistance of Nick Shadow, who clearly represents the Devil. Using eighteenth-century musical and operatic forms (especially Gluck and Mozart), Stravinsky and Auden in effect reinvented the Classical opera of arias, ensembles, recitatives and choruses. The premiere at the Fenice opera house in Venice in 1951 under the baton of the composer himself was a triumphant success, and the choice of Venice indicated once again his close ties with the Italian city. His most important later works – *Canticum sacrum ad honorem Sancti Marci nominis* (1958), and *Threni: id est Lamentationes Jeremias Prophetae* (1958),

both for soloists, chorus and orchestra – were also performed there.

However, the most important aspect of this later period in Stravinsky's creative life is his interest in dodecaphonic music, a compositional technique he had carefully avoided until then. *Canticum*, *Threni* (both entirely serial in conception) and the ballet *Agon* (1957) were the result of his studies of Anton Webern's music in the years from 1952 to 1955.

Old and weary, although intellectually still extremely active, Stravinsky finally revisited Russia. He died on 6 April 1971. In his will he asked to be buried in his adoptive city, Venice, next to his old friend Serge Diaghilef.

Stage		
8 operas	Le Rossignol (The Nightingale)	1908-09
	Renard	1915-16
	L'histoire du soldat	1918
	Mavra	1922
	Oedipus Rex	1926-27
	Perséphone	1933-34
	The Rake's Progress	1948-51
	The Flood	1962
12 ballets	L'oiseau de feu (Firebird)	1910
	Petrushka	1911
	Le sacre du printemps (The Rite of Spring)	1911-13
	Pulcinella (on themes by Pergolesi)	1919-20
	Le chant du rossignol (The Song of the Nightingale, arr. from Le Rossignol)	1917
	Les noces (The Wedding)	1914-23
	Apollon Musagète	1927-28
	Le baiser de la fée (The Fairy's Kiss, after Tchaikovsky)	1928
	Jeu de cartes (The Card Party)	1936
	Scènes de ballet	1944
	Orpheus	1947
	Agon	1956-7

Choral and vocal		
numerous works	including:	
	Le roi des étoiles (The King of the Stars, male chorus and orchestra)	1911-12
	Symphony of Psalms (chorus and orchestra)	1930
	Three songs from Shakespeare (mezzo and piano)	1953
	In memoriam Dylan Thomas (voice, trombones and string quartet)	1954
	Threni: id est Lamentationes Jeremiae Prophetae (soloists, chorus and orchestra)	1958
	Anthem 'The dove descending breaks the air' (unaccompanied chorus)	1962
	Elegy for J.F.K. (voice and three clarinets)	1964

Concertos		
Four works	Concerto for piano and wind instruments	1923-24
	Capriccio for piano and orchestra	1929
	Violin concerto in D	1931
	Mouvments for piano and orchestra	1959

Orchestral		
numerous works	including:	
	Symphony No.1 in E flat	1905-07
	Scherzo fantastique	1907-08
	Feu d'artifice (Fireworks)	1908
	Symphony in C	1939-40
	Danses concertantes	1941-422
	4 Norwegian Moods	1942
	Symphony in Three Movements	1942-45
	Scherzo à la russe	1944

Chamber & instrumental		
numerous works	including:	
	Chant funèbre (Funeral Song) for winds on the death of Rimsky-Korsakov (now lost)	1908
	Ragtime for 11 instruments	1918
	Symphonies of Wind Instruments	1920
	Octet for wind instruments	1922-23
	Duo Concertante for violin and piano	1931-32
	Divertimento for strings	1934
	Concerto in E flat 'Dumbarton Oaks' for chamber orchestra	1937-38
	Ebony Concerto for jazz band	1945
	Concerto in D for string orchestra	1946
	Septet for strings and winds	1952-53

Piano		
numerous works	including:	
	4 Studies, Op.7, for four hands	1908
	Waltz for children	1917
	Piano-rag-music for four hands	1919
	Serenade	1925
	Sonata for two pianos	1944

Solo vocal		
numerous works	including:	
	Souvenir de mon enfance (Recollections of My Childhood)	1906c.
	Faun et bergère (Faun and Shepherdess)	1906
	Pastorale	1907
	Deux mélodies	1908
	Deux poèmes de Paul Verlaine	1910
	Deux poèmes de Konstantin Bal'mont	1911
	Berceuse du chat (Cat's-Cradle Songs)	1915
	Four Russian Songs	1918-19

Shostakovich

The Russian composer Dmitri Shostakovich photographed in his study. Novosti Agency, Rome.

Dmitri Shostakovich was born on 25 September 1906 in St Petersburg into a well-off middle-class family. His father, a chemical engineer, and mother, an excellent pianist, belonged to the increasingly subversive intelligentsia described so well by Turgenev in his novels. Dmitri and his two sisters studied piano with their mother Sophia Vassilevna, and the boy soon began composing. His earliest efforts, *The soldier*, inspired by the war, a *Hymn to liberty*, and a *Funeral march for the victims of the Revolution*, already show the tendency to relate his music to events in the real world that would become increasingly important in his later works.

St Petersburg, and indeed the whole of Russia, was in ferment, gripped by a heady mixture of subversive violence and glorious hope. The famous composer Alexander Glazunof (1865-1936), head of the St Petersburg Conservatory, kept a careful eye on the progress of Dmitri, who had begun his studies there in 1918, and his protection proved increasingly valuable with the political situation deteriorating by the day. The existing famine worsened, and his father died in 1922, leaving his family in a state of total poverty, which made especially welcome the scholarship Dmitri had obtained with Glazunof's help from the Borodin Foundation. His piano playing progressed so rapidly that he came second to Lev Oborin in the Warsaw Piano Competition.

Mino Maccari's stage design for the 1964 XXVII Maggio Musicale Fiorentino production of Shostakovich's "The Nose". Property of the Ente Autonomo Teatro Comunale, Florence.

In the meantime, he had graduated in composition at the Conservatory and had feverishly completed his First Symphony. At its premiere in Leningrad's enormous Philharmonic Hall on 12 May 1926, a capacity crowd rose to its feet to salute the first Russian composer of the Revolution, and the success of the symphony spread outside Russia, with Toscanini, Stokowski and Bruno Walter all including it in their repertoires.

Looking back to those early days, it seems fairly clear why the First Symphony was a such a huge and unexpected success. One reason was certainly its extraordinary vitality, which fuses diverse stylistic and formal elements into a compact and extremely powerful musical statement, uniting the Russian popular tradition with the Western symphonic tradition. In this sense, Shostakovich showed himself to be Tchaikovsky's true heir in the 20th century.

Moreover, the 30 years separating Tchaikovsky's *Pathétique* from Shostakovich's First Symphony were so crowded with wars and revolutions that their historical importance is out of all proportion to their brief temporal span. The well ordered certainty of 19th-century society had been shattered, and with it the love of elegant forms and comforting harmonies in music. The doom-laden prophecies of Expressionism were followed by Cubism in painting and atonality in music. Assailed on all sides, Western artistic and cultural traditions yielded to the violence of Stravinsky's *The rite of spring* and Schönberg's *Pierrot lunaire*.

Shostakovich felt part of a generation that had lived through a victorious revolution, and so instinctively identified himself with the Romanticism of the new age he lived in. Although dissatisfied with his Second Symphony, and Third Symphony (*The first* of may), both of which he quickly withdrew, they do confirm the continuous presence of patriotic and popular elements in his music.

This continuity is nowhere more evident than in his first opera, *The nose*, which failed, however, to impress the audience at its premiere in Leningrad on 12 January 1930, largely because it was musically and politically unpopular, a deliciously (though libellously) irreverent swipe at bureaucracy in all its forms. As Mayakovsky's had done (*The flea* was written during the same period), Shostakovich's satire lashed out in all directions, challenging artistic and social conformity with a Surreal concept of theatre that destroyed convention, eroded the comforting surface of everyday life and reduced narrative to a merry-go-round of apparent absurdities.

'In a context such as this', commented Shostakovich, 'music cannot be regarded as separate from its text, which it comments upon, illustrates and presents. Music plays its part in this subversive game and is drawn forward by a subtle thread of alienation which of its own nature produces gestural provocation and ideological tension'. Although its jazz rhythms, harmonic abrasiveness and idiomatic use of recitative and speech to the detriment of song are

Cover of the score of Shostakovich's Cello Sonata, Op. 40. State Music Publishers, Moscow.

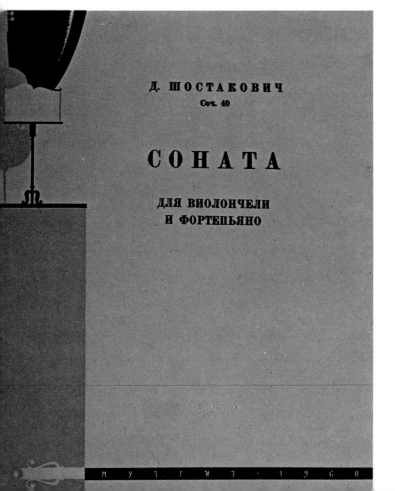

in some ways derivative, *The nose* carries nonetheless the full imprint of Shostakovich's unique musical personality.

During the same period, Shostakovich also wrote incidental music (including music for Meyerhold's staging of *The flea*) and film music, once again showing the interest in linking music to gesture, image and speech that would lead directly to *Lady Macbeth of the Mtsensk district* (1930-32), a crucial landmark in his composing career. This was a turbulent political and social period. The West was in the grip of an economic crisis, and political power in the Soviet Union was gradually concentrating in the hands of a man intent on imposing his iron rule on the country. In the United States, Eisenstein was fighting the producers who wished to stop the filming of his revolutionary epics, in Russia Mayakovsky was on the verge of suicide, and in Germany Hitler was well on his way to becoming an absolute dictator. And yet, there was still room for optimism and hope: the prospect of building the world's first Socialist state in the face of a hostile Europe of coalitions was still an exciting one.

These contradictions are reflected in *Lady Macbeth of the Mtsensk district Katerina Ismailova*, in which Surreal caricature is replaced by hard-nosed and at times abrasive realism. The subject of the opera, taken from Nikolai Leskov's novella published in 1865, is as scandalous as that of *The nose*, although more on account of its brutality (a criminal story of adultery containing three murders and a suicide) than the absurdity and weirdness of the earlier opera. Its dramatic tension lies in the contrast, brilliantly underlined by the music itself, between Katerina's radiantly indomitable character and the oppressiveness of the world she lives in. Once again, the brilliance and originality of the work lies in the quality of its satire, with its references to other avant-garde tendencies of the age, and in this sense there is no real discontinuity between *The nose* and *Lady Macbeth*. What is different, however, is the way in which the structure of *Lady Macbeth* reintegrates the fragments produced by the rebellious destructiveness of the earlier opera. Shostakovich's masterpiece was banned after 100 performances, and never reappeared on the Soviet stage for the next thirty years. Although more succinct, the Fourth Symphony (1935-36) is very much of a piece with *Lady Macbeth*, and it too was savagely attacked in **Pravda**. Between the two came a pair of important piano works, the 24 Preludes, Op. 34, and the First Piano Concerto. Although an outstanding pianist in his own right,

Poster for performances of "Katerina Izmailova" at the opera house in Poznan in 1965. Theatre Museum, Warsaw.

became increasingly difficult because his adherence to the official directives was never total. Like Prokofief, Khatchaturian and other 'non-bureaucratic' composers, Shostakovich refused to accept that the point of contact between serious music and the Soviet masses should be sought in the country's lowest common musical denominator, although he recognised that there was now a totally new audience for serious music, and that real contact with millions of men and women avid for culture was an absolute necessity. Thus, he openly acknowledged the justice of the charges against him, but tried to implement the recommendations of the general directive in an original way, a decision that would lead either to prizes or reprimands depending on the political climate of the moment.

Composed in 1935-36, the Fourth Symphony was the first of a series of large-scale orchestral works in which he returned to the Romantic concept of the symphony as a vehicle for philosophical statement and the expression of personal feelings and states of mind. No other symphonist has come closer to capturing the neurotic anguish and obsession of Mahler, with his constant wavering between triumphant

Cover of the score of Shostakovich's 9th Symphony in D major, Op. 70. Breitkopf und Härtel Musikverlag, Wiesbaden.

Shostakovich had written nothing for the instrument since the First Sonata and *Aphorisms* of 1926-27, and the virtuoso brilliance of the new works reflect a renewed interest in concert performance. He played the 24 Preludes in Moscow on 24 May 1933, and the First Piano Concerto in Leningrad later in the same year, on 15 October, to great public acclaim. Although the Preludes have never really established themselves, the Concerto is now one of the world's most popular works for piano and orchestra.

By 1936, the 30-year-old Shostakovich, Russia's first composer of the Revolution, was now well established both at home and abroad, but it was precisely then that *Pravda* launched a series of vitriolic attacks against the 'modernism' of his music, citing, among other features its absence of melody, the 'triumph of noise', and a 'lack of truth'. *Lady Macbeth* was totally demolished, and it was obvious that the sudden attack had been building up for some time. In the name of Art, and on behalf of the Russian people (for whom it claimed to speak), Russian bureaucracy called for clear, comprehensible works corresponding to Socialist reality rather than sterile games of art for art's sake. Shostakovich's position

Breitkopf & Härtels Partitur-Bibliothek

Nr. 3606

DMITRI SCHOSTAKOWITSCH

Sinfonie Nr. 9

op. 70

VEB BREITKOPF & HÄRTEL MUSIKVERLAG

184

affirmation and crushing defeat. *Pravda* recommended that the work should be withdrawn even during rehearsals, and it was replaced by the Fifth Symphony, described by Shostakovich as 'the creative reply of a Soviet artist to justified criticism'. Its triumphant premiere in Leningrad on 21 November 1937 and immediate popularity abroad can probably be explained by the clarity of its formal structure and the incisiveness and memorability of its themes.

Having satisfied the recommendations of the directive in word if not in deed, Shostakovich proceeded to go his own way in his next orchestral work, the Sixth Symphony, which carries his rejection of Classical forms a step further, most obviously because it abandons the four-movement format of the Classical symphony. The Sixth Symphony, the first of a trilogy of 'war' symphonies, was followed by the Seventh *Leningrad* Symphony composed during the siege of the city, when tens of thousands of people were dying of cold, starvation and repeated bombardment. The symphony is an epic portrayal in sound of civilised man's outrage and anguish at the brutality and futility of war. This theme reaches its fullest expression in the Eighth Symphony, the peak of Shostakovich's symphonic output, in which he establishes a unique balance between form and content, concept and realisation. Monumental in scale as well as in theme, it was first performed in Moscow in November 1943.

Two years later came the Ninth Symphony, the complete opposite of the Eighth, in which a return to a French wittiness and brilliance, at times bordering on caricature (very much in the style of the earlier Concerto for piano, trumpet and strings), seemed to parallel the return of peace to war-torn Europe. Neither the Eighth nor the Ninth met with official approval, however. The 'Zhdanov Report' and subsequent decree on artistic life in the Soviet Union openly condemned all forms of 'Western deviation' and sought to impose an unthinking type of Soviet nationalism in all fields ranging from literature and music to science and art. Poetry, song and even physics and genetics now had to qualify for approval by demonstrating their 'popular' origins in the epic struggles of the Russian proletarian movement.

Systematically enforced by the all-powerful state and party machine that had emerged from the Second World War, this obscurantist nationalism virtually

A photograph of the Beethoven Quartet which gave the first performances of Shostakovich's string quartets. Novosti Agency, Rome.

put an end to musical activity in the Soviet Union. New works that succeeded in slipping through the net of official artistic controls were the exception rather than the rule. Shostakovich managed to publish a number of important new works, however, especially in the field of chamber music. With the First Quartet (1938), the Quintet (1940) and the Trio (1944) behind him, he brought his number of Quartets to ten in the years from 1944 to 1964, and also composed the important *Eleven Jewish Songs* (1955). Of his orchestral works, only the Violin Concerto (1947-48) and the Tenth Symphony seem worthy of mention. The Concerto was first performed by its dedicatee, David Oistrakh, in 1955, and has been very popular ever since. The Tenth Symphony marked Shostakovich's return to the symphony after composing the Ninth in 1945. It is very much an 'in memoriam' work expressing his desperation at the outbreak of war in the Far East and the suppression of civil rights movements everywhere, and his hope for a brighter future in a world dominated by dictators and Cold-War politics.

In this depressing climate, Shostakovich's output also began to deteriorate. Occasional works such as *Song of the forests* (1949) were followed by an Eleventh Symphony (1957), a Twelfth Symphony (1961) inspired by the October Revolution, a Thirteenth Symphony (1962) dedicated to the Jews massacred in Kiev and immediately suppressed by the authorities, an experimental Fourteenth Symphony (1969) and his final Fifteenth Symphony (1971).

Of his vast vocal and instrumental output, the most significant works are the Cello Concerto (1959), the cantata *The execution of Stepan Razin* (1964) and *Seven Pieces for children* for piano (1944-45).

Dmitri Shostakovich died in Moscow in 1975.

Stage			
operas	The Nose	Y. Preis (from Gogol)	1930
	Lady Macbeth of the Mtsensk District (Katerina Ismailova)	Y. Preis D. Shostakovich (from Leskov)	1934
	The Gamblers (unfinished)	(Y.P.& D.S., from Gogol)	1942
	Moscow, Cheremushki		1959
ballets	The Age of Gold		1930
	The Bolt		1931
	Bright Stream		1934
incidental music	The Flea	Mayakovsky	1929
	Hamlet	Shakespeare	1932
	King Lear	Shakespeare	1940
film music	New Babylon		1928
	The Golden Hills		1931
	Maxim's Return		1937
	Vyborg District		1938
	The Silly Mouse		1939
	Zoya		1944

Orchestra	
Symphony No. 1 in F minor	1926
Symphony No. 2 in B major 'October Revolution'	1927
Symphony No. 3 in E flat major 'The irst of May'	1931
Symphony No. 4 in C minor	1936
Symphony No. 5 in D minor	1937
Symphony No. 6 in B minor	1939
Symphony No. 7 in C major 'Leningrad'	1941
Symphony No. 8 in C minor	1943
Symphony No. 9 in E flat major	1945
Symphony No. 10 in E minor	1953
Symphony No. 11 in G minor	1957
Symphony No. 12 in D minor	1961
Symphony No. 13 in B flat minor 'Babi-Yar'	1962
Symphony No. 14	1969
Symphony No. 15 in A major	1971

Concertos	
Piano concerto	1933
Piano concerto No. 2	1957
Cello concerto No. 1	1959

Chamber		
12 String Quartets including:	String Quartet No. 1	1938
	String Quartet No. 2	1946
also	Piano Trio No. 1	1923
	Piano Trio No. 2	1944
	Piano Quintet	1940
	3 Pieces for violin and piano	1940
	3 Pieces for cello and piano	1924
	Cello Sonata	1934
	3 Fantastic Dances for piano	1922
	Piano Sonata No. 1	1926
	10 Aphorisms for piano	1926-27
	24 Preludes for piano	1932-33
	6 Pieces for Children	1944-45
	24 Preludes and Fugues	1951

Vocal	
6 Romances on words by Japanese Poets for tenor & orchestra	1928-31
4 Romances (texts by Pushkin)	1936
Native Leningrad, suite for chorus & orchestra	1942
2 Fables (texts by Krylov) for voice & orchestra	1942
6 Romances (texts by Burns, Shakespeare, Ralegh)	1942
The Song of the Forests, oratorio (text by Dolmatovsky)	1949
Jewish Songs (ancient popular songs)	1955
The Execution of Stepan Razin, cantata	1964

Arrangements	
Tahiti Trot for orchestra	1928
New orchestration of Mussorgsky's 'Khovantschina'	1939-40
Boris Godunov	1963

Gershwin

Photograph of George Gershwin. Photograph by Edward Steichen.

George Gershwin was born in 1898, in Brooklyn, New York, into a modest Jewish immigrant family of middle-class Russian origin. His father had had to try his hand at a number of trades, but there was always enough money in the home to pay for piano lessons for his children, and especially for George, who had his first experience of music on hearing classical music coming from a pianola shop on one side of a street and jazz coming from a club on the other. After his first lessons with a variety of unknown instructors, he began to study with his first real teacher, Charles Hambitzer, a concert artist and operetta composer, who directed his new pupil to the music of Chopin and Debussy. But George was also fascinated by the syncopated rhythms of jazz. By 1913, when he was 15, the classic 'New Orleans'

The "Original Dixieland Jazz Band" photographed in 1917.

style was already known in New York, and the Original Dixieland Jazz Band, a group of White musicians, had already had the honour of being the first band to record jazz music. In fact, it was White musicians who had first made jazz popular, although it was, of course, already well known to America's Black musicians, who played it in a completely different way, however. It was these White jazz musicians, then, who first opened George's eyes to the possibilities of Afro-American music.

Already a competent pianist, Gershwin found work at the age of 16 as a piano player with Remick, the music publisher, in Tin Pan Alley, New York's mythical street of American song. Seated in a small room there, George would play the firm's music for singers, impresarios and musicians on the look-out for new songs that might become hits. The sentimental salon piece was then still the most fashionable type of song, but George quickly realised that times had changed, that the machine age had begun, and that songs would now have to adapt and change. He decided to make a career for himself as a song writer, published his first song in 1919, and got himself known on the Broadway theatre circuit,

with the result that his musical *La, La, Lucille* was mounted in 1919 and soon became a popular success. In the same year, his song *Swanee*, sung by Al Jolson, became a smash hit. Al Jolson was a 'White minstrel' who, by painting his face black on stage, had seemed to capture the essence of the Afro-American spirit for the White population, with the result that his singing made it possible for Black artists to appear in White theatres.

After the end of the First World War, the American musical world was anxious to establish a uniquely American school of twentieth-century composition and performance. The United States was, and still is, a melting pot of races and cultures, and this diversity was reflected in the range of musical styles and idioms it was producing. A special concert was mounted in New York in 1924 at which a jury of non-American classical musicians and academics (including Sergei Rachmaninof, Jascha Heifitz and Alma Gluck) was to rule on 'what American music is'. Gershwin was present at the event with a semi-symphonic 'jazz' piece called *Rhapsody in blue* which he had written in a mere 22 days. The jury failed to comment on the pieces it heard, but the audience

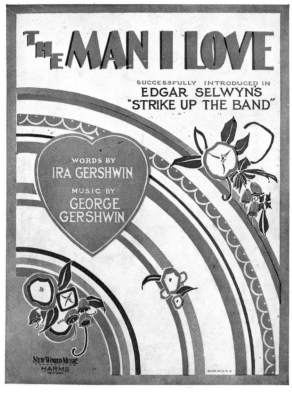

Poster for the performances of Gershwin's musical "Funny Face" at the Princes Theatre in London, 1928.
The Museum of the City of New York, New York.
Top right: title-page of the song "The Man I Love".
Below: title-page of the song "Oh, Lady Be Good".
Museum of the City of New York, New York.

had already made up its own mind, and greeted Gershwin's piece with rapturous applause. Paul Whiteman, the conductor on that memorable evening, was a White musician who had always been attracted to jazz and had been one of America's first

189

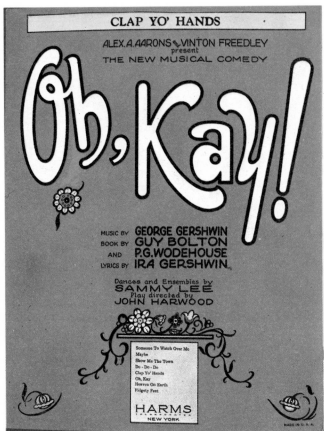

George Gershwin and his brother Ira in a caricature drawing.
Museum of the City of New York, New York.
Poster for the film of "An American in Paris". S.A.C., Milan.
On the left: title-page of the song "Clap Yo' Hands" from the
review "Oh Kay". Museum of the City of New York, New York.

jazz arrangers, although he had little claim to be an authentic jazz performer in his own right. It was he who had encouraged George to compose in the jazz idiom and would subsequently bring his later symphonic works to the attention of the public.

A few Swing tunes and the use of syncopated rhythms are not enough, of course, to turn jazz song and dance into a real concerto for piano and orchestra, but Gershwin had, in fact, written a true virtuoso piece in the semi-academic mould with the added 'colouring' of Afro-American music. It is this which explains the modernity of the piece and makes Gershwin the first really American composer. And yet, throughout his life Gershwin was never convinced that he could write 'real' music, or that he knew music as thoroughly as a true composer should, and this in spite of the musical creativity and genius for melody that never deserted him. He continued to study classical music and sought the advice of composers such as Maurice Ravel and Igor Stravinsky in his constant endeavour to improve his technique. However, during a visit to Europe in 1928 to immerse himself in the musical climate there, all the musicians he approached refused to give him lessons. He was already famous, and *Rhapsody in blue* was being performed in concert halls along with music by Weber, Liszt and Copland.

Between 1924 and 1931 he wrote a series of increasingly successful Broadway musicals, including *Lady be good* (1924), *Oh, Kay* (1925), *Funny face* (1927), *Show girl* (1929), *Strike up the band* (1930), *Girl crazy* (1930), and *Of thee I sing* (1931), but after the success of *Rhapsody in blue* he went on to make an even greater name for himself as a classical composer. Walter Damrosch, conductor of the New York Symphony Orchestra, advised its president, Harry Harkness Flager, to commission a concerto from Gershwin, and the result was the Concerto in F for piano and orchestra. The public declared the work a triumph but the critics were divided, at a loss to know what to make of this 'typical', classically inspired concerto. The Paris premiere of the Concerto in F at the Opéra in 1928, with the composer himself present, was equally successful, but for Gershwin the most important event of this European tour was his meeting with Alban Berg in Vienna. The cultured and refined Austrian, one of the leading dodecaphonic composers of his day, was dazzled by Gershwin's songs, while Gershwin, Berg's exact opposite as a musician, was enraptured by the latter's music, and was delighted to receive a score of his *Lirische Suite* for string quartet with a dedication from the composer himself. Returning from his stimulating tour of the Old World, Gershwin composed another symphonic piece, *An American in Paris*, in 1928, which was followed in 1932 by *Second rhapsody*, even though he continued his hectic involvement in Broadway musical and theatre life. The premiere of the *Second rhapsody*, another variant of the standard concerto for piano and orchestra, was given with the Boston Symphony Orchestra under Sergei Koussevitzky.

A visit to Cuba in 1932 inspired Gershwin to write the *Cuban Overture* on his return. The premiere concert (including other Gershwin pieces) at New York's Lewisohn Stadium attracted an audience of 17,000, a foretaste perhaps of the huge pop concert audiences we are now familiar with. The concert was a

A still from Otto Preminger's 1959 film of "Porgy and Bess" based on Gershwin's opera.

191

triumph, but Gershwin was dissatisfied. He had written five 'symphonic' works, changed the entire idiom of American music, helping at the same time to launch stars such as Ginger Rogers and Fred and Adele Astaire, and had contributed to the development of the film musical after the invention of the cinema sound-track, but he had yet to realise his one great dream: to write an opera.

In 1932, he bought the musical rights to Edwin Dubose Heyward's novel *Porgy*, which had been a publishing hit over the previous few years. Heyward's scenes of suburban life in a Black city fascinated Gershwin, who had never lost contact with the Black music and musicians he had known in his Tin Pan Alley days. In order to absorb to the full the atmosphere of the Deep South, he moved in 1934 to Folly Island outside Charleston, where he lived in a small house with just an upright piano and the bare essentials of life, like one of his own characters in the opera, studying the spirituals and musical life of the common people there. Four years later, his new opera, *Porgy and Bess*, was performed for the first time on 10 October 1935, and went down in musical history as one of the least explicable opera fiascoes of all time. There was, naturally, a good deal of cultural confusion and incomprehension, and neither critics nor public would appreciate Gershwin's music until after his death, when everyone suddenly realised that *Porgy and Bess* was, in fact, the first American opera.

At the age of 38, Gershwin was rich and famous, but as he himself said in 1937, the year he died, he had also been profoundly unlucky.

He went to Hollywood in 1936 to write the sound-track for Shall We Dance with Fred Astaire and Ginger Rogers. All the greatest New York talents – actors, musicians and writers – were now in Hollywood, attracted by the possibilities of sound cinema. It was in the creative turmoil of this tinsel world that Gershwin met the great Viennese composer Arnold Schönberg who had fled there from the Jewish persecutions in Europe.

Gershwin died in 1937 after a sudden illness while working on the sound-track for Damsel in Distress.

Operas		
Title	Librettist	Date & place of 1st perf.
Blue Monday (135th Street)	B.G. De Sylva	29.8.1922 one performance with the musical George White's Scandals of 1922, Globe Theatre, New York
Porgy and Bess	Dubose Heyward & Ira Gershwin	30.9.1935 Colonial Theater, Boston 10.10.1935 Alvin Theater, New York

Solo & Orchestral		
Piano & orchestra	Rhapsody in Blue for piano & orchestra	1924
	Piano Concerto in F major	1925
	Second Rhapsody for piano & orchestra	1932
	Variations on "I Got Rhythm" for piano & orchestra	1834
Orchestra	An American in Paris	1928
	Cuban Overture	1932
Piano	Three Preludes	1926
	Transcriptions of 18 songs	1932

Musicals		
29 musicals including:	Half-Past Eight	1918
	Capitol Revue	1919
	La, La Lucille	1919
	The Scandals of 1920	1920
	The Scandals of 1921	1921
	George White's Scandals of 1922	1922
	George White's Scandals of 1923	1923
	Lady Be Good	1924
	Oh, Kay	1925
	Funy Face	1927
	Rosalie	1928
	Show Girl	1929
	Strike Up the Band	1930
	Girl Crazy	1931
	Of Thee I Sing	1933
	Let 'Em Eat Cake	1933
	Pardon My English	

Cinema		
Films from musicals	Girl Crazy	1929
	Strike Up the Band	1940
	Lady Be Good	1941
	Girl Crazy	1943
Film music	Delicious	1931
	Shall We Dance	1937
	Damsel in Distress	1937
	The Goldwyn Follies	1939
	Rhapsody in Blue	1945
	The Shocking Miss Pilgrim	1947
	An American in Paris	1951